Marriage
Insurance

BY **Willard F. Harley, Jr.**

His Needs, Her Needs

Marriage Insurance

Marriage Insurance

Willard F. Harley, Jr.

Fleming H. Revell
Old Tappan, New Jersey

Library of Congress Cataloging-in-Publication Data

Harley, Willard F.
  Marriage Insurance / Willard F. Harley, Jr.
    p.   cm.
  ISBN 0-8007-1610-8
  1. Marriage.   2. Interpersonal relations.   I. Title.
HQ734.H2853 1988
646.7'8—dc19   88-15304
                                                                      CIP

Copyright © 1988 by Willard F. Harley, Jr.
Published by the Fleming H. Revell Company
Old Tappan, New Jersey 07675
Printed in the United States of America

Contents

PUTTING THE FOUR POLICIES TO WORK

YOUR MARRIAGE INSURANCE

Marriage Insurance

One

Breaking the
Illusion Barrier

A happy marriage seems like an impossible dream to most people these days. Many freely admit that their marriages were disappointing right from the start. Others find happiness for a while, only to find themselves gradually drifting into unhappiness. Still others find their unhappiness growing into unbearable pain and seek divorce as their only hope for relief.

I am writing to men and women who want to build a happy marriage that *stays* happy: A *divorce-proof* marriage. You may have come from a childhood home that was torn apart by divorce. Perhaps you have been divorced yourself and are concerned because statistics show that a high percentage of second and third marriages end in divorce, too. Or maybe you're in a fairly solid marriage but are concerned about the ease with which some people drift into divorce.

Whatever your background or attitude may be toward divorce, you're wise to recognize the great risk of divorce that every married couple faces. And you're even wiser to learn how to *insure* your marriage against divorce.

This book takes a strong stand against divorce. I believe marriage should be for life. *But this book takes an even stronger stand against pain and misery*. Marriage was never intended to be an opportunity for one person to torture and torment another. It's an opportunity to provide a level of care not found in any other human relationship. Divorce is sometimes the only escape from death, crippling injury, or emotional collapse. What begins for many as love, often ends as a nightmare of hate.

I'm not for divorce, but I'm also not for unhappy couples, limping along, painfully, miserably for years. As a psychologist, professional marriage counselor, and Christian, I see the need for doing more than telling couples to avoid divorce. People need to be shown how to change attitudes and beliefs that *lead to* divorce. These attitudes and beliefs lie buried, like seeds, in almost every one of us. If they are allowed to grow, they can destroy a marriage.

The Illusions of Marriage

Over the years I've heard couples tell me how disillusioned they are with marriage. Their disillusionment begins with a false understanding, an illusion. It shouldn't surprise you that young adults have certain misconceptions about marriage. But what may surprise you is that, for many, the very root of these illusions lies within the words of our traditional wedding ceremony.

Imagine for a moment that you are seated in a sunlit church at the wedding ceremony of two friends. The minister faces the bridegroom, before this audience of witnesses, and asks:

> Will you take this woman to be your wife, to live together in the holy covenant of marriage? Will you love her, comfort her, honor and keep her, in sickness and in health, and, forsaking all others, be faithful to her so long as you both shall live?

The groom responds, "I will." The bride also agrees to this same declaration of consent.

Then the minister asks the groom to repeat the marriage vows. The bride repeats them also, saying:

I take you to be my husband, to have and to hold from this day
forward, for better or for worse, in sickness and in health, to love
and to cherish, until we are parted by death; as God is my witness,
I give you my promise.

As powerful and inspiring as these promises are, they do not
keep good, loving, well-intentioned men and women from
winding up at the office of a divorce attorney. In fact, they tend
to create in us illusions that leave us unprotected from some of
the most common causes of divorce. I would like to consider
these illusions one at a time.

The First Illusion: Care given and received in marriage is unconditional.

Is it true that I will cherish my wife until we are parted by death
no matter what she does to me or for me? Can I expect my wife
to care for me no matter how I treat her?

I want to believe that my wife will care for me unconditionally.
I feel insecure with the understanding that if I treat her badly,
she'll end her commitment to me and divorce me. I want her to
tell me that she'll always care for me, even if I don't care for her.

Women who do fulfill this commitment are sometimes beaten,
verbally abused, and victims of infidelity. If I truly care for my
wife, however, as I vowed when we were first married, *I will not
want her to remain married to me if she is hurt by the relationship.*
I ought to want her to *leave me* if I no longer treat her as I should.

Most men and women break their marriage commitment
when they come to recognize that their efforts to stay married are
ruining their lives. Most divorces are not the result of two people
simply drifting apart. More typically divorce is the result of
people hurting each other so badly that one or both cannot
endure the relationship any longer.

The Second Illusion: Romantic love is permanent.

The feeling of romantic love is by far the most important
criterion people use to select their life partners. The feeling is so

strong, they cannot imagine ever losing it. So it seems reasonable to promise their love for life.

At the time of marriage most people do love and cherish one another. The wedding vows accurately describe their present feelings, which include the false impression that their feelings will not change.

But that extraordinary feeling of love, the feeling of passion and romance that guides people in selecting their life partner, can sometimes evaporate after only a few years of marriage.

The feeling of love is less permanent than most people would like to believe.

The reason this feeling changes is that it's an emotion, and *all* of our emotions change and evolve. They are often reactions to our environment. As we have control over our environment, we are able to exert some control over our emotions. But none of us can simply *decide* to feel a certain way, because our environmental control is usually quite limited.

Perhaps you've noticed that it is impossible to remain happy for weeks at a time. Something always comes up that wrecks your good mood. In the same way, our feeling of love is just as volatile. Feeling in love depends on factors over which we have very little control. The most important of these is how well your spouse meets your marital needs. In other words, your spouse has more control over your feeling of love than you do!

And there are some factors that are beyond *both* you and your spouse. You may lose your feelings of love through no fault of your spouse at all. For example, many of my clients who suffer from chronic depression report falling "out of love" during a depressive episode. The state of depression colors all other emotional states and temporarily eliminates all good feelings, including love for your spouse.

I may want to think that my wife, Joyce, will feel in love with me forever, but the facts convince me that she has very little control over it. She simply cannot commit herself to loving me, because she alone cannot do it. My care for her, among other things, will decide how much she'll love me.

The Third Illusion: A husband and wife should love and accept each other as they are, and not try to change each other.

One pervasive romantic ideal is that we are loved for who we are, and not for what we do. I suppose all of us want that kind of love for ourselves (it's a lot less work!), but we shouldn't forget that those we love have done something very meaningful to us. And the one we pick as our life partner has done an incredibly good job of meeting our needs, at least at the time we were married.

Because we want to be loved for who we are, we're somewhat offended when people suggest that their love is conditional on what we do. When we're asked to change our behavior, we sometimes feel, "If you really liked me, you would look beyond my behavior and accept me as I am."

It's easy for us to forget that whenever we show *care* for someone, we're changing our behavior to meet their needs. So when someone asks us to change our behavior to accommodate them, that person is simply asking for our care.

At the time most people are married, they choose partners who meet the marital needs of a healthy, happy, young adult. They do not consider the needs of middle age, sickness, parenting, emotional distress, or the many other events of a lifetime.

Some become disillusioned when they discover that the person who was just perfect for them at age twenty is no longer compatible with their needs at age fifty. Needs that were unknown when a couple began having a family become apparent at the time children are grown and move away from home.

While many new needs are predictable at these points in a person's life, especially to professional marriage counselors, the *sense* of need does not arise until the change actually takes place.

For example, most women have a need for husbands to take an interest in their children. But until children arrive, a woman might find herself very satisfied with her husband. There has not yet been an opportunity for him to please or disappoint her in this need. After the children are on the scene, however, her need becomes apparent, he fails to fulfill that need, and she finds herself with a marital crisis of major proportions.

Another related problem is that a person's good intentions are sometimes not enough to satisfy ordinary needs. For example, a woman may agree at the time of marriage to meet her husband's sexual needs only to find that in practice she finds sex disgusting and degrading. She may go through her entire lifetime with attitudes and habits that leave her husband sexually unfulfilled.

A man who is chronically unemployed poses for his wife the same sort of dilemma. During the first few years of marriage, his wife sees his unemployment as little more than a difficulty in adjusting to the right job. But after many years she comes to realize that he simply does not like to work as much as most other men. He wants to please her and will take jobs for a while just to show her that he loves her. But eventually he quits or is fired because he hates the work so much. It's only then that his wife realizes he will probably never be able to support their family unless he takes radical measures to resolve the problem.

Problems such as these often lead to divorce, not because of failure to be *committed*, but rather failure to be *able* to meet the most important marital needs. But it's important to remember that *inability* can be changed to *ability* if people are willing to change as an act of care and submit themselves to the training that it takes to make the change.

The Realities of Marriage

In view of these powerful illusions, I've constructed three principles based on the realities of marriage. These will be used to guide our thinking throughout this book.

The First Reality: The agreements made in marriage are conditional. Care is given when it is received.

Sometimes the conditions of marriage are not clear at the outset, but they become clearer as the marriage develops. The commitment of care that a husband makes toward his wife assumes that she will care for him also. And when that reciprocal care is not forthcoming, the commitment of care is broken. Most people feel justified to stop caring when they feel uncared for.

The wife who feels uncared for thinks, *Why should I keep giving and giving to my husband, when he isn't putting the smallest effort into this marriage? Besides, if I keep doing things for him, without him doing anything for me, it rewards his inconsiderate behavior!*

It's true! Unconditional care tends to reward inconsiderate behavior. Most of us have noticed that doing nice things for our spouses does not *necessarily* improve their behavior toward us. They appreciate our kindness but don't necessarily repay us with kindness.

When one partner fails to meet the other's needs, it does not automatically break the relationship. At first, the spouse who is offended tries to help the failing partner keep up his or her end of the bargain. But if it's interpreted as unjustified criticism, and the effort fails, the relationship is usually destroyed, because the offended spouse stops caring.

The Second Reality: We have very little control over our feelings of romantic love and cannot guarantee them throughout marriage. To a great extent, our spouses control those feelings.

The feeling of love a couple has entering marriage is precious and easily destroyed. It should be guarded carefully and not taken for granted. While none of us can guarantee our own feeling of romantic love, couples can do many things to protect and encourage its growth.

A host of factors build romantic love, and a host of factors destroy it. We can do something about some of these factors, while others are outside of our control. This book is about the factors we can do something about.

When you make a commitment to treat your spouse with dignity and respect, learning to meet his or her needs, you will have gone a long way toward guaranteeing your spouse's love for you! But your spouse will need to make the same commitment if you expect to return the feeling of love.

The Third Reality: Marital needs change over a lifetime, and old abilities may not meet new needs. New needs often require new abilities.

Most of us are prepared for the needs of our spouse at the moment we are married. We prove it during courtship.

But after marriage, almost immediately, marital needs begin to change. When we make a commitment to care, "for better or for worse," we sometimes assume that we'll be doing the same things in good and bad times. However, caring, particularly in bad times, may require the learning of new abilities to meet the new, sometimes unexpected, needs of your spouse.

While marital needs change, the change is usually predictable. Before children arrive, the needs of affection, conversation, sexual fulfillment, recreational companionship, physical attraction, and admiration usually dominate. But after children, the marital needs of family commitment, financial support, and domestic support become much more important to a couple. Many marriages are ruined when men and women are unwilling to adopt new roles in marriage that accommodate new needs.

In addition to the predictable development of new marital needs, most of us will need something *special* from our spouse during the course of our marriage, something neither they nor we could have anticipated. Our ability to adjust to those special needs often dictates the ultimate success of our marriage.

So far, we have looked at illusions that dictate the policies by which we govern our marriage commitments. By turning those illusions around we have taken a new look at the realities of marriage. As we analyze these realities, it's possible to write new policies for marriage that will lead you to happiness and fulfillment as a couple.

Before we look at these policies, I want to introduce you to the concept I call the Love Bank. The Love Bank is an idea I developed that will help you understand more about your feeling of love. It also helps explain why a good marriage works and why a bad marriage fails. And it will help me explain my new policies for marriage to you.

It's important to understand how the illusions of marriage help deplete one's Love Bank accounts, even when a couple begins their marriage with compatibility and commitment. Policies that take the realities of marriage into account reverse that trend and help build Love Bank accounts.

Two

Your Love Bank: Deposits Only, Please

You were born with a Love Bank. It's a concept I created to help those I counsel understand how their love for others is created and destroyed. Each person you know is automatically assigned his or her own "account." And every experience you have with people affects the balances in their accounts. All this goes on inside you without you ever thinking about it consciously. Here's how it works.

Building a Love Bank Account

Let's say you meet a man for the first time—we'll call him Carl—and he is polite and pleasant. The meeting is a nice experience, and a few "love units" are deposited into Carl's new account. As you leave him that day you think, *What a nice guy. I hope I see him again.*

The next time you hear from Carl, he's on the phone inviting you to play golf with him on Saturday. You think to yourself, *He must like me, too.* You agree to go with him, and a few more love units are deposited into Carl's account.

Not only does your Saturday turn out to be terrific, but you and Carl become regular golf partners. If you're a man, he may add enough to his Love Bank account to become a good friend. But if you're a woman, he may have the potential for making very substantial deposits, enough to make you feel "in love."

From this simple illustration, I hope you can now see how the system works. When you associate a good feeling with a person, love units are deposited into the Love Bank. But bad feelings cause love units to be "withdrawn" from the account.

Once in a while, your feelings are *so* good or *so* bad that many love units can be deposited or withdrawn in a single encounter. Most of the time, however, your feelings are neutral, neither good nor bad, so the accounts of most of the people you know don't change very much.

Whenever a person has made substantial deposits and has a large account of love units, you feel "in love" with that person. To set an arbitrary gauge for comparison, let's say that when a person achieves one thousand love units, it triggers that "in love" feeling in you. A smaller account causes you to simply "like" that person. You "dislike" people when their accounts are in the red, when they have withdrawn more love units than they have deposited. And you "hate" people who have made substantial withdrawals, building huge deficits.

Depleting a Love Bank Account

Let's continue using our fictional friend, Carl, to illustrate how a love bank can be depleted of love units. During one of your golf matches, you confide in Carl, telling him about a personal problem with which you've been struggling. He listens, nods understandingly, and assures you he will hold your problem in complete confidence.

A week later you learn he's shared your problem with others at the golf course. You are embarrassed and angry. Love units are immediately withdrawn from Carl's account, and more love units are withdrawn each time you recall the offense. If you think about it enough, he may lose all the love units he ever gained, and more besides! From that one negative experience, you may come to dislike Carl.

The most volatile accounts usually belong to those with whom you've had romantic relationships, because the feelings you experience are more extreme. When things are going well, hundreds of love units are poured into the account in a short period of time. When things are going badly, however, hundreds of love units can be withdrawn. We rarely, if ever, feel "in love" with someone that we have not been attached to romantically, because it is only these individuals who can build up so many love units so quickly. But the same people can lose love units just as fast.

When a married couple's relationship starts a downward slide, the love loss actually gains momentum, and they begin to hate each other more than anyone they have ever known. Love units are being withdrawn almost continually, because every action is seen as damaging and is resented. The end result may even lead to violence. I have counseled both the victims and perpetrators of violent attacks, and the difference is often only a matter of strength and opportunity. In many cases, their roles could easily have been reversed, since they hated each other so much.

In most marriages, however, the anger that results from an insolvent Love Bank takes more sophisticated forms: criticism, defiance, stubbornness, thoughtlessness, name-calling, and other types of rude behavior. It gets the job done, since the purpose of physical, emotional, and verbal violence is all the same—to make the other person miserable. And the sad fact is that we are more likely to hurt our spouse than anyone else when our Love Bank is depleted. What a tragedy!

People who tire of the ridicule sometimes divorce each other and end the misery. Those who feel that divorce is not a choice open to them run the risk of storing ever greater Love Bank deficits. I've reviewed cases of murder and attempted murder involving people who do not believe in divorce.

My first, best, and strongest efforts go toward trying to prevent divorce. I have come to realize, however, that if the drain of love units cannot be stopped, normal people can become monsters, and divorce can sometimes save lives. I try to prevent divorce by building love, not by forcing people to endure the pain and tragedy of hatred.

The secret to a happy marriage, of course, is to avoid losing love units and to learn how to deposit them. To help you understand how the Love Bank works in the life of a normal couple, I will illustrate the rise and fall of the Love Bank accounts of Sharon and Mike, who are composites of several couples I have counseled.

In this account, as in all references to the Love Bank, the numbers of love units are not to be considered scientifically accurate. They are simply intended to help you understand how the feeling of love is created by acts of care and concern and destroyed by destructive habits.

Whatever Happened to Sharon and Mike?

Sharon was ten when her parents finally ended their marriage. It was a disaster of monumental proportions. Each day was a nightmare, far worse than the fighting and sadness that her parents had endured for as long as she could remember. She felt incredibly alone and rejected, punished for childhood disobedience in a most final and devastating way. She never quite recovered from the feeling that her parents had divorced her, instead of each other.

Sharon's parents' divorce had a major impact on her. At the age of ten, she began to think of ways she could avoid divorce in her own life. She remembered how cold and unaffectionate her mother was, so she vowed to be a very affectionate wife. She remembered how her mother never took interest in any of her father's business activities, so she vowed that when she was married she would talk to her husband regularly about his work.

Her mother would complain about all sorts of things. Sharon vowed never to be a complainer. She made lists of resolutions in her diary that she thought would protect her from divorce.

Mike fell head over heels in love the first time he met Sharon. Even though they were both in the seventh grade, he decided within a week that he would marry her. Sharon was not quite so impressed with Mike. After all, he was three inches shorter than she. But by the time both were in high school, Mike started looking and acting more mature. Sharon noticed that her girlfriends wished he would date them, and he had grown six inches. She decided to give him a chance.

Mike blew the first date. He was so nervous that he couldn't think straight. But Sharon gave him credit for trying, knowing that it was one of his first dating experiences. She gave him another chance.

The second date was the charm. Mike was able to pull himself together and act natural. Sharon had a terrific time. They were both off and running.

Sharon already had built a large account in Mike's Love Bank, because whenever Mike looked at her, deposits would pour in. And this had been going on for three years! Mike, on the other hand, had not impressed Sharon in the same way, so his account in her Love Bank started with almost nothing in it. So at this point, their Love Bank accounts looked like this:

Sharon's balance in Mike's Love Bank. 1,874 love units
Mike's balance in Sharon's Love Bank: 12 love units

Mike felt he was in love, even though they had not been dating very long. No one he had ever known had compiled so many love units in his Love Bank.

Since Mike was absolutely crazy about Sharon, he treated her with the greatest respect and care. Over time love units accumulated in his account, and she became more and more attached to him. She dated other guys once in a while, but they were not

nearly so attentive to her as Mike, and eventually Mike had more
love units than anyone *she* had known. Of course, whenever she
dated someone else, she lost some love units in Mike's Love
Bank, because it made him feel terrible. But she had so many to
begin with, that it didn't noticeably affect his feelings toward her.

By the time they graduated from high school, their Love Bank
accounts were still at uneven levels:

> Sharon's balance in Mike's Love Bank: 2,842 units
> Mike's balance in Sharon's Love Bank: 1,249 units

Mike was more in love with Sharon than Sharon was with
Mike, but they didn't know it. However, since neither one had
ever felt this much in love before, it wouldn't have mattered to
them.

Testing the Waters

When they both graduated from high school, Mike asked
Sharon to marry him.

"Oh, Mike, I'd love to!" she responded. "But I'm afraid that
our feelings might change toward each other and we'll be
divorced, just like my parents."

Mike was sure that would never happen, but he was sensitive
to her fear. "You don't need to decide right now. But I can tell
you one thing. If we're married, I'll never divorce you, and you'll
never want to divorce me!"

Sharon relaxed a little. "Let's wait at least two years, Mike. By
then we'll know better what we want out of life. That should be
a good test of our compatibility."

Their first year out of school was a growing experience for both
of them. Sharon's account in Mike's bank rose to 4,572 love
units, while Mike's account with Sharon crept up to 2,078 units.
Mike was still more in love with Sharon than she was with him.
But remember, anything over 1,000 love units makes a person
feel in love. So with these high numbers, no one really cares

who's ahead. They were both deeply in love, and that's all that mattered to them.

The second year was better than the first. They learned to budget, and both had been given raises at work. They were the very best of friends and had learned to spend their free time together. They shared more and more interests: music, sports, movies, camping. Almost anything one of them wanted to do, the other was willing to try. Their Love Banks accumulated many deposits with very few withdrawals.

When they began to explore marriage more seriously, a neighborhood minister provided premarital counseling. They were encouraged to love each other unconditionally, something that seemed effortless at the time. So without any reluctance on either part, they were married.

Beginning the Voyage

The wedding was a great event. Those who knew Sharon and Mike best felt that if they couldn't make their marriage work, no one could. They were perfect for each other.

At the time of their marriage their Love Bank accounts were:

Sharon's balance: 5,753 love units
Mike's balance: 2,457 love units

Mike expected the honeymoon to be a great vacation. But Sharon expected it to be the most romantic experience of her life: cards, flowers, overflowing expressions of love. It turned out to be Mike's great vacation, but not Sharon's romantic experience. He had a fantastic time visiting Maya ruins, scuba diving, collecting shells, and learning to speak a little Spanish. Sharon was a real champ in joining him cheerfully, so she gained 186 love units. Sharon didn't say anything because it would have ruined their honeymoon, but she was very disappointed. It cost Mike 85 love units.

Once they returned home and settled into a daily routine,

Sharon couldn't understand what was happening to her. After the wedding everything had changed. All at once she expected more of Mike than she did before the wedding. Day after day, week after week, Mike was losing love units. He had never before lost love units for failing to kiss Sharon when they said good-bye. She would kiss him, but her initiative just wasn't the same. She wanted *him* to take the initiative. And she was offended when he hurried out or just forgot.

Sharon was still very much in love with Mike, however, and thought she was being silly to expect Mike to be more romantic than he had ever been. So she never said anything, but the love units kept dropping.

Clouds on the Horizon

One day Mike came home with exciting news. "I've been offered a new job! One of my company's suppliers asked me to become their manufacturing representative. They'll pay me $35,000 a year to start. Isn't that great?"

Sharon was delighted! "Oh, Mike! That's great. When do they want you to start?"

"As soon as I can leave my job. I'm giving my notice tomorrow."

Mike was off and running in a very rewarding career opportunity. But he was into the new job no more than a week, when a serious problem materialized. He discovered that if he was to do the job right, he would have to be out of town three nights a week. Sharon had never lived alone before and knew that being alone was going to be very hard on her. But it was a great job for Mike and she wanted him to be successful, so she was willing to try to adjust to his new schedule.

The first week was terrible for Sharon. She really hated being alone at night, to say nothing about missing him. She cried every night. Then when Mike came home to tell her about all his adventures, she had an incredibly difficult time showing any enthusiasm. But her mother had never shown any interest in her father's work, and Sharon had vowed never to make that same mistake. She listened patiently while he recounted his experiences, but she didn't tell him how unhappy her time had been.

Months passed. Then years. Because Mike was happy with his job and in his relationship with Sharon, she was still building up love units in his account. But he was losing love units every week in Sharon's Love Bank.

By the time Sharon was pregnant in their fourth year of marriage, their Love Banks looked like this:

Sharon's balance: 6,452 love units
Mike's balance: 516 love units

Sharon's love for Mike was dropping to a point where she knew she still liked him, but the feeling she had at one time was no longer there. She had heard that after marriage, passion leaves everyone, and so she assumed that her feelings were normal. She did not know the truth—that passion only leaves those whose Love Banks are depleted, and that she was experiencing a precipitous drop in Mike's love units.

Mike, on the other hand, was more in love than ever with Sharon. And when she told him that she was carrying their first child, he was ecstatic. He also realized that if he were to be a good father, he could no longer be away three nights a week. With careful planning and a few lucky breaks he was able to fulfill his work commitments and avoid overnight obligations. By the time their first child arrived, he was home every night.

Patching Holes in a Leaking Ship

Now that Mike was home on a regular basis, Sharon found that she felt distant toward Mike. She was happy that he tried to help care for little Susan, but he wasn't really all that helpful, and now that he was home he tried to make love more often.

Making love just didn't feel natural to Sharon anymore. It was more of a responsibility. It had been two years since she had experienced a climax, and now she was even having trouble being sexually aroused. Most of the time she faked it. But one night she broke into tears while making love.

Mike had no idea what the problem was. At first Sharon wouldn't tell him. But after she calmed down, she explained how she'd been feeling.

"I don't know how to tell you this," she said hesitantly, "but I used to think that having you at home would be the greatest. Now that you're here, I'm not very happy. You're putting a lot of pressure on me."

"When has sex ever been pressure? If you don't feel like it, just say you don't feel like it. It's that simple." That's what Mike said—but inwardly he was devastated.

Sharon was relieved. "Okay, Mike. From now on, when I really don't feel like making love, I'll tell you."

By this time, Mike had only 267 love units left in Sharon's Love Bank, not nearly enough for her to feel like making love to him. Once in a while she felt guilty enough to go through with it. Over the next five years, they made love very seldom, but often enough to have two more children.

During that dismal period, Mike became more and more upset with Sharon's reluctance to make love, and for the first time in their relationship, she was losing love units from his Love Bank. He was still sensitive, however, and while he didn't gain very many love units with Sharon, he didn't lose very many either.

After their third child was born, their Love Banks looked like this:

Sharon's balance: 2,358 love units
Mike's balance: 314 love units

The fatigue and lack of privacy that accompany three small children gave Sharon a good excuse to put off her husband's sexual advances. She didn't think of them as excuses at the time, because Mike had told her clearly that if she was not in the mood to make love, she should tell him. But the real reason that she was never in the mood was that she had lost her feeling of love for him. And she could never tell him that.

The Ship Is Sinking

One night Mike came home from work late after stopping for a few drinks. He was drunk. Sharon had already gone to bed, and as he stumbled into the bedroom, he woke her up with loud complaining about their stalled sexual relationship. "I'd make a good priest! I've learned the secret to celibacy—all you have to do is be married to a woman like you."

"Mike, be quiet! You'll wake the children," she said angrily.

"I've decided that men should have sex whenever they want it," he continued. "If they wait for women, they'll wait their life away. Isn't that right, Sharon?"

"Mike, I'll talk to you about this in the morning, when you're sober. Go to bed."

"No, I think that the time has come to take matters into my own hands."

He forced himself on Sharon. It was one of the most ugly experiences of her life. She didn't want the children to know what was happening, so she endured the humiliation and pain with tears.

The next morning, Mike was frantic. He had no idea that he was capable of committing such a disgraceful act. In tears, he begged Sharon's forgiveness. But the damage had already been done. She did not want him to touch her. For the first time in their marriage, Mike's love units had fallen under zero. As I explained earlier, too many painful experiences can push a person's account into a negative balance. And when that happens, we experience feelings of dislike or even hatred.

At this point, their Love Bank accounts were:

Sharon's balance: 1,746 love units
Mike's balance: − 217 love units

Sharon disliked her husband. Mike made matters worse by getting involved sexually with Peggy, a fellow employee. She had already been attracted to Mike, so when he confided to her that he was having trouble with Sharon, she let him know that she was available. They began an affair.

It seemed like a great short-term solution. Mike's need for sex was met, and he actually felt much less resentment toward Sharon. Partly because of guilt, he bought Sharon token gifts, took her out more often, and set aside more time to be with his children. All of these things helped build love units. Within a few months, his account was in the black again. Sharon forgave him for raping her when he was drunk, and their relationship seemed to be headed in the right direction. She also started to make an effort to improve their sexual relationship. He saw his marriage improve, and discreetly ended the affair with Peggy.

Things were on track for the first time in quite a while. They started to understand each other's feelings more deeply and learned to respond to each other's needs more effectively. That is, until Sharon received an anonymous telephone call.

"I can't tell you who I am, Sharon," said the hushed voice, "but I feel you should know that your husband has been unfaithful to you. The other woman's name is Peggy _____."

With that, the caller hung up.

Sharon was shaking. Her skin crawled. At first, she thought it might have been a crank call, but the more she thought about it the more concerned she became.

When Mike came home that evening, Sharon asked disinterestedly, "Who is Peggy _____?"

That sure got his attention. He turned pale as he stammered a reply.

"Uh, well, I think she's a sales representative that works the south side. Why do you want to know?"

Sharon could tell that she'd struck a nerve. "Do you know her very well?"

"No, not really. Why are you asking these questions?"

"Have you ever gone out to dinner with her?" she persisted.

Mike knew that she knew something, but he didn't know how much. "Why? Did someone tell you we had dinner together? I may have had dinner with her; I can't remember all the people I have dinner with. What is this all about?"

Sharon's face was reddening. "You've had more than dinner with her, haven't you?"

He couldn't look her in the eye. They had been so honest with each other lately, and their relationship was improving so much. Should he continue to lie, or tell her the truth? He took a deep breath. "Sharon, you're being ridiculous. This is beginning to upset me." Then he turned and left the room.

It didn't take Sharon long to find Peggy's telephone number in the directory. She dialed, and in a moment a woman answered. "Peggy, this is Sharon, Mike's wife. Mike just told me that you and he have had an affair."

"Well, Sharon, what can I say? The world isn't always the way we want it to be. But if it's any consolation, it was over several months ago. We're finished."

"How long did it last?"

"Ask Mike; he's got the big mouth!" Then Peggy hung up.

Sharon was devastated. As far as she was concerned, any hope of having a decent marriage had just been smashed. Love units were being withdrawn by the carload. She didn't tell Mike what she had learned.

While he was at work the next day, Sharon moved herself and the three children to her mother's. Peggy happened to see Mike at work and expressed dismay that he would have told his wife about their affair.

"I didn't tell her anything," Mike shot back. "She was asking a lot of questions yesterday, but I denied everything. Did you tell her something?"

"Oh, Mike, I blew it!" Peggy replied. "She called me last night and said you had confessed everything. I assured her that it was over. I even called you a big mouth."

"Man, am I in trouble!"

Mike rushed home to find his family gone.

For the next few weeks, Sharon was inconsolable. At first she wouldn't even speak to Mike. When she finally did, she called him every name imaginable. After several shouting matches, Mike was finally disgusted and resigned himself to a cold war of undetermined length.

When Sharon finally returned home, four months later, their Love Banks had these balances:

Sharon's balance: 1,128 love units
Mike's balance: −758 love units

The only reason that Sharon came back to Mike was to avoid a divorce. Her children had been just as upset as she had been when her parents divorced, and the advice of her mother was to give her marriage a second chance. But once she was home, her feelings toward Mike were unbearably negative. Everything he did irritated her.

Mike was still in love with Sharon, but she was beginning to hate him. She remembered how critical her mother had been, and now she began to understand why: Her mother had come to hate her father and couldn't help herself. Sharon realized that the same thing was happening to her. Venom would pour from her lips whenever she and Mike were together for any length of time.

Manning Separate Lifeboats

Mike and Sharon both decided, independently, that the only way they could stay together for the sake of their children was to develop separate lives. They learned to live in the same house, enjoy their children together, but have minimal conversation when alone. They made love very seldom. Sharon hoped that somehow, over the years, she could regain the feeling she once had for Mike. It never happened. Mike waited for the children to grow up and leave home. Then he filed for divorce.

At the time of Mike and Sharon's divorce, their Love Bank accounts were:

> Sharon's balance in Mike's Love Bank: −378 love units
> Mike's balance in Sharon's Love Bank: −857 love units

Neither Mike nor Sharon made any effort to restore the relationship because they had both come to dislike each other. Sharon actually hated Mike and was relieved to have their relationship end. They could not imagine ever loving each other again and were ignorant of the role of their emotions in deciding the fate of their marriage.

Both Mike and Sharon were capable, attractive, well-meaning people, who let inadvertent acts, small lies, and a lack of communication deplete their Love Banks. The great tragedy is that they *would* have been able to rebuild their Love Bank accounts—but they didn't understand how to do it, and they didn't believe that their feeling of love would ever return. All their best intentions, sincere vows, and honest efforts failed to overcome the effect of the Love Bank on their behavior. The Love Bank determined that they would be married; and the Love Bank determined that they would be divorced.

*   *   *

If the Love Bank really determines both marriage and divorce, and I have ample evidence in the thousands of couples I've counseled, it becomes tremendously important to understand how to control Love Bank accounts. This book will tell you how to build up those Love Bank accounts and how to prevent them from being depleted.

In the next four chapters of this book, I'll introduce you to four of the most important principles you'll ever learn: Four Insurance Policies for Successful Marriage. By investing in the kind of marriage insurance I'm going to recommend, you greatly reduce the risk of divorce because they help you maintain and build high Love Bank accounts. It will also help you avoid illusions and disillusionment so common in today's marriages.

In the remainder of this book, we'll see how these policies apply to some of the most common marital problems. Some are simpler, more common. Others are more difficult.

I can promise you this: No matter what your marriage is like right now—good or bad—its outcome is in the hands of you and your spouse. You have the power to build a stronger, more loving, more fulfilling marriage.

Let's begin.

Four Insurance Policies for a Successful Marriage

Three

The First Insurance Policy—
Honesty

Once she was divorced, Sharon looked out her apartment window and reflected on the events of her life. She had such good intentions. She thought: "I did everything I could."

In spite of her best efforts Sharon was alone at forty-three. There was a new man in her life, but she didn't respect him and trusted him even less. And yet she couldn't bear the thought of being alone the rest of her life. How could she have avoided this mess?

I believe that Sharon did the best she could with the information she had. But her efforts, however sincere, were misdirected. Her marriage could have been successful if she had known what makes a marriage work. Ignorance, not lack of effort, was her ultimate downfall.

In this chapter I'll introduce you to the first of four Insurance Policies for Successful Marriage. If you lay down the ineffective and unrealistic expectations couples so often live by and replace them with these policies, love units will be deposited throughout your married life.

To help you remember the four policies, I've given each a single name. They are: Honesty, Protection, Care, and Time. For each policy name there is a policy definition that will appear in a box. Under each policy definition, there are several additional definitions of the policy that help you understand it more completely.

The First Policy, Honesty, gives married couples the information that they need to solve marital problems and enrich the relationship.

The Second Policy, Protection, keeps love units from escaping the Love Bank.

The Third Policy, Care, builds love units into the Love Bank.

The Fourth Policy, Time, keeps a busy schedule from encroaching on the time needed to apply the first three policies.

Let's consider the first of these policies, Honesty. Without it the others won't work. This is the place to begin building a successful marriage.

Honesty

Reveal to your spouse as much information about yourself as you know: Your thoughts, feelings, habits, likes, dislikes, personal history, daily activities, and plans for the future.

This policy can be broken down into five main parts:

1. *Emotional honesty:* Reveal your emotional reactions, both positive and negative, to the events of your life, particularly to your spouse's behavior.
2. *Historical honesty:* Reveal information about all of your personal history, particularly events that demonstrate personal weakness or failure.

3. *Current honesty:* Reveal information about the events of your day. Provide your spouse with a calendar of your activities with special emphasis on those that may affect your spouse.
4. *Future honesty:* Reveal your thoughts and plans regarding future activities and objectives.
5. *Complete honesty:* Do not leave your spouse with a false impression about your thoughts, feelings, habits, likes, dislikes, personal history, daily activities, or plans for the future. Do not deliberately keep personal information from your spouse.

To some extent this rule is something like motherhood and apple pie. Who would dare argue that it's *not* a good idea to be honest? But in my years of experience as a marriage counselor, I have constantly struggled with dishonesty in marriage. Moreover, some counselors advise dishonesty, of all things!

I want to build a case for complete honesty, since there are many situations in marriage where *dis*honesty is the easier way out.

Let's take a careful look at each of the five parts of this policy in light of Mike and Sharon's story.

1.   Emotional Honesty

Reveal your emotional reactions, both positive and negative, to the events of your life, particularly to your spouse's behavior.

When Sharon was dating Mike, it wasn't very difficult to be completely honest with him. They both placed a great deal of value in their ability to express feelings to each other. But they had so many things in common that negative feelings were unusual, and that made honesty much easier. Whenever one of them disagreed with the other the difference was minor, and accommodation was almost effortless.

But during their honeymoon, Sharon was dishonest for the first time in their relationship. She was deeply offended by the way Mike treated her, and she did not tell him how badly she felt. Instead, she told him that she had a terrific time. Love units were lost, and *no adjustment was made to prevent future losses.*

Sharon developed a habit of providing Mike with misinformation about her feelings. His job was very hard on her because she was left alone three nights each week. But she didn't want him to worry about her, so she let him think she was happy with the arrangement. More love units were lost.

When they had children, many adjustments should have been made. Neither Sharon nor Mike was satisfied with the way their life was developing. But they thought it was wrong to complain. They each knew the other was working hard and trying to do his or her best. As dishonesty increased, their love units decreased.

Mike found his sexual relationship with Sharon to be more and more unfulfilling. But he understood the pressure she was under and how tired she was when he came home from work late at night. It was not fair for him to expect her to respond to him just because he happened to have a sexual need at the time. So he didn't tell her that he was becoming more and more sexually frustrated.

Without Honesty, You're Flying Blind

One of the most important reasons that honesty is a basic requirement for a successful marriage is that *it enables a couple to learn to make appropriate adjustments to each other.* Without the facts on the table, an otherwise happy couple can become very unhappy as the events of life turn against them.

All of us must recognize that the circumstances that led us into a happy marriage are going to change over the years. With that basic understanding, we can then see that a long-term happy marriage requires a considerable number of adjustments on the part of both husband and wife. Those adjustments cannot be made unless both parties honestly explain their feelings to one another. Any complaints on either part need to be taken very seriously.

If Sharon had told Mike how his behavior was affecting her on their honeymoon, for instance, he could have made an adjustment that would accommodate her. If he had told her that he was becoming dissatisfied with their sexual relationship, it would have provided an opportunity for her to make an adjustment to him.

While some couples may fail to make a successful adjustment after feelings are honestly explained (my second and third policies deal with that problem), failure is guaranteed when the need for adjustment is *never* communicated.

Persistence Pays

It's unfair to Sharon to say that she *never* told Mike how she felt. When Mike was away three nights a week, she did say on occasion, "I'm feeling lonely."

Mike reacted a little defensively, saying, "Well, I don't know how we can pay these bills if I don't work."

Because she didn't pursue the subject, Mike thought that Sharon had solved the problem. But Sharon hadn't solved the problem. She simply thought that she should not pursue the matter further. She told him how she felt, and if he wanted to do something about it, he would.

Mike also suggested once that they try to improve their sexual relationship, but Sharon explained that the children made her too tired at night. Mike dropped the subject, even though the problem was still bothering him.

These two illustrations demonstrate the importance of persistence. The commitment of honesty does not end when one has reported a feeling. The commitment of honesty is something that a couple must continue to express to each other until the problem is resolved. In other words, for honesty to have taken place in this relationship, Sharon should have confronted her husband with her loneliness on a regular basis because she was lonely on a regular basis. Mike should have done the same with his sexual frustration.

The commitment to honesty means that feelings are openly expressed, whether or not the problem is resolved or whether or not it seems resolvable. Honesty must continue through the resolution of each problem.

As I mentioned earlier, your emotional reactions are a gauge of whether or not you are making a good adjustment to each other. If you feel good, no adjustment is needed. If you feel bad, a change is indicated.

It is very difficult for some people to openly express negative reactions. They may fear that their reactions will be interpreted as criticism. Or they may be critical of their own reactions, telling themselves that they should not be feeling the way they do. They may want to be unconditionally accepted by their spouse and consider their own negative reactions as proof of their own inability to be unconditionally accepting. Whatever the reasons, many couples try to avoid expressing negative emotions.

Both Sharon and Mike were annoyed by each other's developing habits, yet they failed to clearly communicate to each other those negative feelings. As a result, neither of them made the necessary adjustments to accommodate each other. Before long, they had lost compatibility.

While positive reactions are easier to communicate, many couples have not learned to express these feelings either. This failure misses an important opportunity to *deposit* love units. Whenever your spouse has made you feel good, learn to express that feeling clearly and enthusiastically!

2. Historical Honesty

Reveal information about all of your personal history, particularly events that demonstrate personal weakness or failure.

While many people feel that embarrassing experiences or serious mistakes of the past should be forgotten, most psychologists recognize that these are sometimes signs of present weakness. For example, if a person has ever had an affair, he may be vulnerable to another affair. If someone has ever been chemically dependent, he is vulnerable to drug or alcohol abuse in the future. By expressing past mistakes openly, your spouse is able to understand your weaknesses, and together you can avoid conditions that tend to create problems for you.

No area of your life should be kept secret. All questions asked by your spouse should be answered fully and completely. Periods of poor adjustment in your past should be given special attention. Those previous conditions should be more carefully understood, since problems of the past are commonly problems of the future.

Not only should *you* explain your past to your spouse, but you should encourage your spouse to gather information from those who knew you in the past. I have encouraged couples who are considering marriage to meet with several significant people from each other's past. It's often a real eye-opener!

I carry this rule of honesty about the past all the way to the disclosure of all premarital and extramarital sexual relations. My position on the subject of honesty in marriage is that a man and a woman *must* confide in each other regardless of the consequences. Many couples have come to see me and, in confidence, the husband or wife will tell me they have been involved in an affair. I recommend that they explain the situation to their spouse at their earliest opportunity. While these disclosures sometimes lead to months of emotional turmoil, they create the environment needed for the solution to marital problems. In my experiences as a counselor, I've never seen such disclosures, by themselves, lead to divorce.

Dishonesty leads to divorce. Honesty is the first step toward healing. If a couple tries to resolve their conflicts without honesty, what they begin to discover is that significant pieces are missing and there is a lack of true understanding of each other.

3. Current Honesty

Reveal information about the events of your day. Provide your spouse with a calendar of your activities with special emphasis on those that may affect your spouse.

After six years of marriage, Mike discovered that it was easier to have a sexual relationship with a woman at the office than with Sharon. As a result, Mike found Peggy to be a welcome solution to his sexual frustration. He was able to be alone with her several times a week, and their sexual relationship was fulfilling.

Mike justified this infidelity by assuming that he was doing Sharon a favor by not imposing his sexual requirements upon her. Whenever Sharon wanted to make love to him, he was happy to accommodate her, but she didn't feel a sexual need more than two or three times a month. Mike didn't *want* to share information about his daily activities with Sharon, since it would have exposed his relationship with Peggy. The revelation would have completely ruined any hope of continuing this very satisfying solution. Moreover, the announcement of this relationship would have been very upsetting to Sharon. He loved her very much and did not want to put her through the grief of such a disclosure. So in order to preserve a temporary solution to his problem and to keep Sharon from experiencing intense emotional pain, he felt that dishonesty was justified.

In good marriages, couples are so interdependent that sharing a daily schedule is essential to their coordination of activities. But in weak marriages, couples are reluctant to provide their schedules, because they are often engaged in an assortment of relationship-damaging behaviors. They may know that a spouse would object to their activities, and so they tell themselves, "What they don't know won't hurt them."

Even when activities are innocent, it's extremely important for your spouse to understand what you do with your time. Be a person who is easy to check up on and easy to find in an emergency. Give each other your daily schedule so that you can communicate to each other how you spend your time. Once married, almost everything you do will affect your spouse. Therefore, it is important to explain what you do each day.

4. Future Honesty

Reveal your thoughts and plans regarding future activities and objectives.

One time I was counseling a couple who were in their second marriage. Barbara had three small children when she married Ed and was delighted to have help raising them. But soon after the marriage, Ed became inconsiderate to her. She decided to remain married only until her youngest was eighteen. Sure enough, on her youngest child's eighteenth birthday, she filed for divorce. Ed was devastated! He had not been given a clue that Barbara was planning the divorce. According to Barbara's reasoning, as long as she met Ed's needs while they were married, he was compensated for his help in raising her children. Once his job was completed, she had no reason to continue meeting his needs.

Another couple I knew, but didn't counsel, had a similar problem. He married her because he needed financial support through graduate school. During their marriage he did his best to be a loving and caring husband, but once he received his doctoral degree, he divorced her. He felt that he had been fair, since while she was supporting him financially, he was also meeting her needs.

The secret plan to divorce in each of these cases was not an isolated instance of dishonesty. These couples did not discuss future plans *in general*. They may have discussed minor plans or made careless attempts at discussing major plans, but careful thought about the future would not have made sense. Why put time and energy into thinking about something you know you won't be doing anyway?

If these couples had been in the habit of discussing future plans, the truth would likely have been revealed. And even though they were married for the wrong reasons, the truth would have given them a chance to reassess their resources. They might have made a successful adjustment.

In most marriages, however, the failure to explain future plans is more innocent. Some couples do not explain their plans to each other because they do not want to change them if the spouse expresses a negative reaction. They feel that explaining a future plan may "prepare the evening for war," and the spouse will be successful in scuttling the plan.

There are many reasons why you may not want to explain your plans to your spouse. But the result is always the same: Your spouse will not know the truth. And without the truth, none of us is able to use our considerable resources of intelligence and creativity. We cannot cope with the problems of life if we don't have the truth.

This brings us to the last part of this policy.

5.   Complete Honesty

Do not leave your spouse with a false impression about your thoughts, feelings, habits, likes, dislikes, personal history, daily activities, or plans for the future.

Do not deliberately keep personal information from your spouse.

In general, my policy of honesty, the first policy for marital success, is designed to create mutual understanding. If you or your spouse do not wish to be understood, you cannot expect to experience a successful marriage.

It goes without saying, but I'll say it anyway: False impressions are just as bad as outright lies! The purpose of honesty is having the facts in front of you. Without the facts, you will fail to solve the simplest marital problems. Why should it make a difference how you fail to reveal the facts to each other, whether by lies or by leaving false impressions? Either one will leave your spouse ignorant.

I need to ask probing questions during premarital counseling. I know the areas where people tend to leave false impressions, and I ask pointed questions in each of these areas. Since most marital problems originate with serious misconceptions, I do what I can to reveal them. In most cases, the biggest false impression is that your spouse is doing a good job of meeting your needs. The truth is that, in some areas, you're very unsatisfied.

Why do people leave false impressions? Sometimes to protect feelings. When exposed, feelings are often hurt. But that is no reason to leave false impressions. You *cripple* your spouse when you fail to reveal the truth.

*   *   *

Honesty is a necessary first step in solving marital problems. But honesty alone is not enough. There are three more policies that need to be activated as you pursue a successful marriage.

The next chapter introduces the second policy: Protection. It helps you prevent the loss of love units.

Four

The Second Insurance Policy—
Protection

When Mike married Sharon, he was so much in love that he couldn't imagine ever losing that feeling. As far as he was concerned, he would be in love with her the rest of his life. Sharon had felt the same.

But on the day they were divorced, all the love they'd once had for each other was gone. Where did it go? How did it go?

This chapter covers the policy that has the greatest effect on *maintaining* love units. It shows you how to avoid losing the love units that made your marriage possible.

Protection

Do not be the cause of your spouse's
pain or discomfort (unless it is unavoidable
to follow the policy of Honesty).

As with the first policy, I've divided this one into several parts to make my intentions clearer:

1. *Protection from anger:* Never punish your spouse; never curse, make disrespectful judgments, or lecture through

verbal reprimand; express anger as a feeling, not as an
instrument of vengeance. Never *intentionally* hurt your
spouse.
2. *Protection from annoying habits:* Do not persist in
inconsiderate habits or activities. If your spouse tells you
that one of your habits or activities is annoying, change
it to accommodate your spouse's feelings, or stop doing
it. Avoid *unintentionally* hurting or annoying your
spouse.
3. *Protection from demands:* Do not demand anything of
your spouse that would cause pain or discomfort. When
requesting a favor, ask how your spouse feels about
doing it and, if the response is negative, withdraw the
request.

This policy is harder to justify than the first. While almost
everyone agrees that violence is to be avoided, I have trouble
convincing people that statements of disrespect, annoying habits,
or demands also have *no* place in a successful marriage. (Let's see
if I can convince you.) We'll start with the easy part that covers
expressions of anger.

1.   Protection from Anger

**Never punish your spouse; never curse, make disrespectful
judgments, or lecture through verbal reprimand; express anger as
a feeling, not as an instrument of vengeance. Never *intentionally*
hurt your spouse.**

One of the last things that Sharon ever thought she'd do is *try*
to hurt Mike. She had seen her parents hurt each other and had
promised herself that no matter what happened she would never
treat her own husband the way her mother treated her father.
And yet, after Sharon discovered that Mike had been unfaithful
to her, she was so angry with him that she felt she had a right to
punish him.

Mike came to her in tears, begging her to forgive him and
promising never to become involved with another woman again.

But Sharon was not willing to forgive him quite that easily. She lost her temper with him on numerous occasions, calling him degrading and humiliating names.

Finally, Mike had enough of all this and started blaming Sharon for his indiscretion. He told her that if she had behaved like a normal woman, he would never have been tempted by someone else and that her sexual problems ultimately led to his affair. He told Sharon that Peggy was ten times the woman she was and that their sexual relationship was only a small part of a wonderfully fulfilling relationship. He knew that these accusations would hurt Sharon deeply, and when he said them he didn't really care. But later, he always regretted what he had said.

Following each of these temper tantrums there would be a period of making up where each of them would claim not to have meant what he or she said and that it was only said to hurt the other person. The truth was that they were being partially honest when they were fighting. The way they expressed their feelings, however, was designed to hurt the other person. They *intended* to punish each other as they were expressing their deepest resentment.

Do you ever find yourself in word battles like this with your spouse? Do you needle or try to tear each other apart with your words?

It's important to recognize that fighting, like the kind just described between Sharon and Mike, is *not* what I mean by honesty. Honesty is the expression of feelings without blame or judgment: It's telling someone that you're unhappy, without saying that it is the other person's fault.

Only God Has the Right to Argue

An argument is quite different from the honest sharing of feelings. In an argument, people say that they are unhappy—but they also attempt to prove they are right and the other person is wrong, or that the other person needs to change before he or she can be "right." An argument changes the simple expression of feelings to moral indictment. After trying to prove yourself "right" and your spouse "wrong," an argument then moves to the next step: meting out appropriate punishment.

Many arguments represent a conscious and deliberate attempt to degrade and humiliate the person that you have promised to "love, protect, and defend." Even if your spouse hurts you, you must promise not to hurt your spouse in return. You must keep yourself from intentionally and deliberately humiliating, degrading, or hurting your spouse in any manner.

It's a sad commentary on the state of marriage that we find so many cases of wife beating. If men were to follow the principle of protection, there would be no physical abuse of women. There is no good excuse for one spouse to hit another. While men are most often blamed for abuse of women, it is just as important to recognize that women should never slap or hit their husbands either. Even though they may not be strong enough to do him any physical damage or emotional harm, physical attacks have no place in a healthy marriage. It's a measure of how low respect, caring, and communication can get.

Sometimes punishment is subtle. To avoid retaliation, people may mask punishment as an unintended mistake. A wife may "forget" to pick up her husband after work, or a husband may leave the car at home without any gasoline. The policy of protection includes such subtle forms of punishment as these. Never deliberately do anything to cause your spouse pain or discomfort, even if it could not be known that you planned it.

Any time you intentionally punish or hurt each other, you are raiding each other's Love Banks. Love units are lost. You not only suffer from the pain of the punishment itself, but also from the hurt feelings that you have when the one who is supposed to love you most turns on you.

Why would couples do something to deliberately destroy their love? In most cases they don't understand what they're doing. They think they are "teaching" each other a lesson, letting each other know what it feels like to be hurt. Besides, they think that their love will not be affected by the punishment, because they agreed to love each other forever! But they are very, very wrong. The wedding vow means nothing in practice; the Love Bank means everything. And they are destroying carefully built, but delicate, Love Bank accounts.

What if you discover that you can't control yourself? You dislike your spouse so much that you find yourself criticizing everything he or she does, or you knowingly try to be hurtful. My recommendation is that you get help from a professional counselor. Don't allow yourself to be abusive, and don't allow your spouse to be abusive to you.

✻   ✻   ✻

The second and third parts of this policy of protection are more difficult to explain to people than the first part. So I need to begin with a statement of the principle implied in the rule of protection:

NEVER GAIN AT YOUR SPOUSE'S EXPENSE

If you ever find pleasure in something that brings pain or discomfort to your spouse, you must avoid it entirely.

This principle has far-reaching and critical implications in a marriage. It says, simply, that it is more important to prevent your spouse's loss of love units than for you to be happy.

One illustration of how this works is described in what is called a *zero-sum game*. In this type of game, every point you win is a point lost by your opponent. You each begin the game with no points, and as one of you gains points, the other is losing them. When you have 15 points, he has -15 points; when you have -8 points, he has 8 points. At any time during the game, the sum of your points and those of your opponent is always zero.

Many marriages are like zero-sum games. For one to gain, the other must lose. Today, we do what I want and you must suffer through it. Tomorrow, we do what you want and I must suffer through it. *The policy of protection clearly states that zero-sum games are out.* Unless you both win, you can't play the game. Unless you are both happy, you must think of something else to do.

In order to understand the full implications of this principle, we will look at the remaining two parts of the policy of protection. This may be tough, so hang on!

2.   Protection from Annoying Habits

Do not persist in inconsiderate habits or activities.

If your spouse tells you that one of your habits or activities is annoying, change it to accommodate your spouse's feelings, or stop doing it.

Avoid *unintentionally* hurting or annoying your spouse.

Sharon knew long before she married Mike that a few of his habits irritated her considerably. One such habit was the way he sat in a chair. She admired men who would sit straight and tall. It made her feel that they were alert and attentive. When a man slouched in his chair, it reminded her of certain relatives for whom she had no respect. When Mike would come home and slouch in a chair to watch television, it bothered her a great deal and he lost love units in her Love Bank. Once in a while she would mention it to him. He would straighten up and continue watching television with a better posture, but a day later she found him back in the same slouched position. More love units were lost.

Many couples who see me for counseling want to know if they have the right to try to change each other. On one hand, they notice things they would like to change. On the other hand, they don't want to seem too critical and don't want to crush part of their mate's identity.

It's important for all of us to realize that annoying habits are not a part of one's character or identity. They have developed randomly over a period of time for unimportant reasons.

Some habits are relatively easy to overcome. For example, if a woman is disgusted with her husband's personal hygiene, he can learn, without too much difficulty, to take a shower and wash his hair daily, brush his teeth at least twice a day, wear clean clothes, and be clean shaven. Women are often annoyed by habits like spitting on the sidewalk, using coarse language, and telling offensive jokes, habits which some men see as inoffensive.

A characteristic female habit that many men find irritating is long telephone conversations on evenings when their husband is at home. Perhaps the wife does not initiate the phone call, but rather a friend calls to talk. She doesn't want to be rude and spends some time talking to that friend. Five minutes later, another friend calls and she spends some more time on the phone. By the end of the evening, three or four friends have called, she has spent anywhere from fifteen minutes to a half-hour with each of them, and her husband has been ignored. When her husband expresses his irritation, it's very difficult for her to see that she is gaining at his expense. Unless she changes that habit, she'll lose love units in her husband's account.

In short, a habit that seems okay to you but annoys your spouse must go. If not, love units go!

3. Protection from Demands

Do not demand anything of your spouse that would cause pain or discomfort. When requesting a favor, ask how your spouse feels about doing it, and if the response is negative, withdraw the request.

Demands are often presented with implied threats of punishment. "If you refuse me, you will regret it." In other words, "I know you'll feel bad doing what I demand, but if you don't, you will feel even worse." This is a clear example of playing the zero-sum game—and playing to win! But you'll lose love units with certainty.

In most marriages demands are common. People expect certain needs to be met in marriage, and when they find reluctance in their spouse, they tell the spouse that they have no choice in the matter. They must do what is needed or bear the consequence, which is punishment. This, of course, is a violation of the policy of protection because the reluctant spouse has a good reason for being reluctant.

When I ask my wife to do something for me, and she refuses, it is because she would not enjoy doing it. More to the point, she would dislike it! I may justify my request by insisting that it is her responsibility. But that justification overlooks the policy of protection: Never cause your spouse discomfort.

Some men might ask, "But what if she loafs around the house all day? What if she goes out with her friends every night? What if she leaves me with the kids all the time? What then?"

I'd say you have a serious problem. But *demands* will not solve that problem. You cannot force your spouse to meet your needs. They are either met willingly from a commitment of care, or they will not be met. Threats, lectures, and other forms of manipulation do not build compatibility; they build resentment.

Your Spouse Needs Protection from *You*

You may notice that the rule of protection is not intended to guard your spouse from the dangers of life: Instead it guards your spouse from the dangers of *you!* You are the most serious threat to your spouse's happiness. There is no one with as great a potential for causing your spouse serious harm and lifelong misery as you. Many divorces are the result of one spouse trying to escape sadistic and brutal punishment by the other. Even annoying habits have driven many to divorce.

We all have the seeds of love and hate, good and bad, care and destruction within us. We must learn to guard our spouses from the impulses of harm that creep into relationships—impulses of self-centeredness that make my happiness more important than the happiness of my spouse.

Very often, one of the very first steps in helping a couple reconcile is to teach them to stop hurting each other. I forbid arguments of any kind. I forbid physical and verbal attacks. I forbid demands on each other. I make every effort to teach each person to try to accommodate the other so that they do not offend, annoy, or hurt each other.

It's only when people learn to protect each other that they are in a position to care for each other. And that leads us to my third policy for successful marriage.

Five

The Third Insurance Policy—
Care

When Sharon and Mike were married, the most clearly understood part of their wedding vows was that they would care for each other throughout their lifetime. They understood that care is more than a feeling, it's a commitment to make every reasonable effort to meet each other's needs.

While they were still dating, Mike would tell Sharon that if she married him he'd make her the happiest woman in history. She'd be the center of his life and his world would revolve around her. Sharon knew that if the marriage was to work she had to treat him the same way. She had to make him happy as well and make every effort to meet his needs.

While they each had the right intentions and the correct understanding of care as a marital commitment, they did not understand how difficult it would be to *learn* to care for each other. They both thought care was something you could decide to do, and once the decision was made, caring would become spontaneous.

That was not the case. Spontaneous acts of caring rarely come naturally. Therefore, my third policy needs to be adopted.

Care

Learn to meet your spouse's most important marital needs.

Again, I've divided this rule into three parts to help clarify its meaning:

1. *Identify marital needs:* Identify your spouse's marital needs, and select at least five that are most important to your spouse, those that are likely to bring the greatest marital happiness and fulfillment.
2. *Meet marital needs:* Create a plan to help you learn to meet your spouse's five most important marital needs.
3. *Reassess needs and effectiveness of need fulfillment:* Evaluate the success of your plan, creating a new plan if the first is unsuccessful. If your spouse finds that a new marital need has replaced one of the original five, learn to meet that new need.

Care is the *willingness* to change your own personal habits for the benefit of the person you have chosen to marry, and then *making sure* that those habits are changed. These changes in habit do not cause anyone to lose their identity or to become a robot. Our habits are very often developed through chance and are not necessarily a reflection of our character or our major goals in life.

However, the process of discarding old habits and developing new ones is difficult and stressful. This is one reason that well-intentioned couples often fail in their efforts to learn more accommodating habits. It's not only difficult for us to change for our spouse, but it is also difficult to put our spouses through the stress of making changes to accommodate us.

Sharon and Mike thought they were compatible when they

were married. They got along with each other extremely well and felt that they were made for each other. It did not occur to them that after marriage new marital needs would develop.

Care is more than learning to meet another's needs at a point in time. It also requires the willingness and ability to meet changing needs.

One of the more common reasons for divorce today is that a husband and wife have "grown apart from one another." One of them may have completed an education while the other one did not. One of them may have developed new career interests and the other did not join in those interests. Very often, children impact on the interests of a couple and send them in different directions.

I believe that growing apart is the result of failure to continue learning how to care for one another. Instead of learning how to meet each other's needs, couples assume that their instincts will carry them. When their instinct seems to fail, they conclude that they must be incompatible. Growing apart means that a couple has not grown in compatibility. They have let nature take its course, and the new needs that are inevitable in marriage are left unmet because no effort was made to create new habits to meet them.

Extramarital affairs and multiple marriages represent one strategy in adjusting to the failure to create compatibility. Over a period of time, as needs change and a relationship falls apart, a new relationship may be created with another individual who, by chance, is prepared to meet the new needs that have developed. But we have an enormous capacity for adjustment. Learning to meet each other's marital needs is far less complicated than going through the agonizing ritual of divorce and remarriage.

The first part of my third policy, care, focuses attention on the need to know where you're going.

1.   Identify Marital Needs

**Identify your spouse's marital needs, and select at least five that
are most important to your spouse, those that are likely to bring
the greatest marital happiness and fulfillment.**

I've written an entire book on this subject. The book, *His
Needs, Her Needs* (Revell, 1986), identifies the most important
marital needs for men and women and teaches couples how to
develop habits that meet those needs.

Discovering your spouse's marital needs is made difficult by
the fact that the marital needs of men and women are often very
different, especially the ones that are the most important. This
difference often confuses and complicates the problem, because
men try to meet needs most important to men and women try to
meet needs most important to women. Thus, they often fail to
meet each other's real needs.

When the best efforts of a man and woman go unappreciated,
and their own needs are not met, they often give up trying. If they
had only directed their efforts in the right places, they would have
been effective and appreciated.

I want to review the ten most important marital needs,
identified in *His Needs, Her Needs*. While all ten are important,
five of these needs are of critical importance to most men, and
the other five are of critical importance to most women. All of
these categories may not apply to your marriage. But they can
help you begin a discussion with your spouse to identify the needs
you should learn to meet.

A man's five most important needs in marriage are:

1. *Sexual Fulfillment.* She meets this need by becoming a
   terrific sexual partner. She studies her own sexual
   response to recognize and understand what brings out
   the best in her; then she shares this information with
   him, and together they learn to have a sexual relationship that both find repeatedly satisfying and enjoyable.

2. *Recreational Companionship.* She develops an interest in the recreational activities he enjoys most and tries to become proficient in them. If she finds she cannot enjoy them, she encourages him to consider other activities that they can enjoy together. She becomes his favorite recreational companion, and he associates her with his most enjoyable moments.

3. *Physical Attractiveness.* She keeps herself physically fit with diet and exercise, and she wears her hair, makeup, and clothes in a way that he finds attractive and tasteful. He is attracted to her in private and proud of her in public.

4. *Domestic Support.* She creates a home that offers him a refuge from the stresses of life. She manages household responsibilities in a way that encourages him to spend time enjoying his family.

5. *Admiration.* She understands and appreciates him more than anyone else. She reminds him of his value and achievements and helps him maintain self-confidence. She avoids criticizing him. She is proud of him, not out of duty, but from a profound respect for the man she chose to marry.

When a man is married to a woman who has learned to meet these needs, he'll find her to be irresistible. These needs are usually essential to a man's marital happiness.

A woman's five most important needs in marriage are:

1. *Affection.* He tells her that he loves her in words, cards, flowers, gifts, and common courtesies. He hugs and kisses her many times each day, creating an environment of affection that clearly and repeatedly expresses his love for her.

2. *Conversation.* He sets aside time every day to talk to her. They may talk about events in their lives, their children, their feelings, or their plans. But whatever the topic, she enjoys the conversation because it is never judgmental, always informative and constructive. She talks to him as

much as she would like, and he responds with interest. He is never too busy "just to talk."

3. *Honesty and Openness.* He tells her everything about himself, leaving nothing out that might later surprise her. He describes his positive and negative feelings, events of his past, his daily schedule, and his plans for the future. He never leaves her with a false impression and is truthful about his thoughts, feelings, intentions, and behavior.

4. *Financial Support.* He assumes the responsibility to house, feed, and clothe his family. If his income is insufficient to provide essential support, he resolves the problem by upgrading his skill to increase his salary. He does not work long hours, keeping himself from his wife and family, but is able to provide necessary support by working a forty- to forty-five-hour week. While he encourages his wife to pursue a career, he does not depend on her salary for family living expenses.

5. *Family Commitment.* He commits sufficient time and energy to the moral and educational development of the children. He reads to them, engages in sports with them, and takes them on frequent outings. He reads books and attends lectures with her on the subject of child development so that they will do a good job training them. He and she discuss training methods and objectives until they agree. He does not proceed with any plan of training or discipline without her approval. He recognizes that his care of the children is critically important to her.

Of course, these categories do not apply to everyone. Some men look at their list and throw two out to make room for two from my "woman's needs" list. Some women do the same. Belief that these categories are right for everyone is a big mistake! The reason that I suggest them, however, is to help a couple start the process of identifying what they need most in marriage. It is simply a way of helping them think through what it is that makes them happiest and most fulfilled. I also want couples to realize that what a man needs in marriage is usually quite different from what a woman needs. That makes the whole process of discovering your need very personal; it's something you must do for yourself. Then you should explain your discovery to your spouse.

Once you feel you understand your most important marital needs, you are ready for the second part of the policy.

2.   Meet Marital Needs

Create a plan to help you learn to meet your spouse's five most important marital needs.

Learning to meet your spouse's most important marital needs usually requires literally hundreds, maybe thousands of new habits. But the habits all come together eventually to form a whole. It's like learning a part in a play: You begin by learning each line, each motion, each cue, but eventually it comes together as a whole. It's naturally whole; it doesn't seem like hundreds of little pieces.

Let's take a look at one of Sharon's marital needs: affection. There were many habits that Mike should have learned to meet this need, but because he didn't understand its importance, he let opportunities to deposit love units slip away.

For instance, Mike did the grocery shopping because the store was on his way home from work and he didn't mind doing it. One day Sharon suggested that he buy a particular brand of orange juice that she liked. To her surprise Mike came home with the same brand he had always bought.

"Why did you buy this orange juice?" she asked.

"Oh, it's a little less expensive," he replied.

She was disappointed and took his forgetfulness as lack of care. He felt very foolish and later admitted that he'd simply forgotten. He'd get her brand the next time.

The following week, Mike went to buy the groceries and came back again with the less expensive brand of orange juice. He was in the habit of buying a certain brand and had difficulty remembering Sharon's request. He was also unaware that the change would have met one of her marital needs: affection. She would have interpreted the purchase of her brand as an expression of love for her, a way of saying, "I love you." He, on the other hand, thought it was simply buying orange juice.

From that day on she never mentioned anything more about orange juice, but every time Mike came home with that inexpensive brand he lost an opportunity to deposit love units.

We Are All Creatures of Habit

People who study human behavior—psychologists—are acutely aware of how much our behavior depends on habits. As human actors we think that we behave spontaneously, with freedom to express ourselves any way we choose. But this feeling is an illusion. The truth is that we are very much creatures of habit.

Day after day we do the same things over and over. Psychologists learn how to predict our behavior by simply observing it and assuming that it will repeat itself.

When we want to change our behavior, we should set into motion a procedure that is designed to replace an old habit with a new habit. That procedure is not completed in a single effort. In order to establish a new habit we must repeat a certain behavior over and over again. And that behavior must be followed by what psychologists often call *reinforcement*. A reinforcement is nothing more than a reward or good feeling for having behaved a certain way.

We'll use the case of Sharon's orange juice to help explain the steps necessary to change a habit. You'll probably object to the fact that this procedure takes the romance out of buying orange juice. Bear with me. I'll explain later how romance can still play a role.

> *Step 1: Define the desired behavior.* In this case, Sharon wants Mike to buy a certain brand of orange juice and not buy other brands.

Step 2: Be certain that the behavior is performed. Telling Mike to buy a certain brand was not sufficient to guarantee the purchase. She might have to write him a special note. *Step 3: The behavior must be reinforced.* Upon his purchase of the new brand of juice, he must then be reinforced (rewarded) for the new behavior. She must simply tell him how much she appreciates his thoughtfulness and encourage him to continue to buy the same juice in the future. *Step 4: Continue monitoring the behavior until it has become a habit.* It should not surprise Sharon if, after the next shopping trip, she finds the inexpensive orange juice in the grocery bag. It would simply reflect the fact that the old habit is still present. She should ask Mike to return to the grocery store and make an exchange. After he completes this pilgrimage she should give him a big hug and tell him how much she appreciates him working on this small but important habit. Habits often take months to establish, but once in place they are usually effortless to maintain.
Step 5: Evaluate the success of your plan, creating a new plan if the first is unsuccessful. If Sharon were to find that Mike continued buying his brand of orange juice after all her efforts, she should not give up on the project. Instead she should create a new plan.

You're probably thinking that I've missed the point. You're thinking, "Sharon didn't want the orange juice as much as she wanted Mike to show that he *cared* for her. Once he's *trained* to buy a certain brand, it's no longer affection, it's just a habit."

But I haven't really missed the point. I've come to realize that marital needs must be met on a continuing basis, and the affection that comes from a habit feels just as good as spontaneous affection that comes from a momentary feeling—and it's more reliable! The affection people really need in marriage comes in the form of habits, not attitudes. While we all want to be loved, love does us no good if it just remains a feeling. It must be followed by action.

I'm sick of hearing how much an alcoholic husband loves his

wife the day after he slapped her around and verbally abused her. He keeps hanging on to the strange notion that his feeling of love is doing her some good. If that's love, who'd want any part of it?

On the other hand, I've counseled many couples in which a man has developed habits of affection, yet he has *lost* the feeling of love. His wife still loves him dearly because he meets her needs, even though his feeling of love is gone, and she knows it.

I maintain that affection is *learning* to do things that communicate care. If Mike had learned to buy Sharon's brand of orange juice, he would have created love units, because his new habit would have made her happy. The fact that she may become a part of his learning process does not discount the value of the new habit or the positive effect it will have on her.

Each marital need involves the development of hundreds of new habits. Each habit builds love units, but the more there are, the more each habit is worth. At some point, your spouse will feel complete in your ability to meet the most important marital needs. When that happens, love units pour in!

The last part of this policy reminds you that as your spouse's needs change, your habits should change to keep pace.

3. Reassess Needs and Effectiveness of Need Fulfillment

Evaluate the success of your plan, creating a new plan if the first is unsuccessful. If your spouse finds that a new marital need has replaced one of the original five, learn to meet that new need.

Think of marriage as a big fish net that is stretched across a river. Each day the fisherman comes by, takes the fish caught in the net, and sells them at the market. But along with fish, branches and other debris are caught in the net.

There are three kinds of fishermen.

The first fisherman only takes the fish and lets the debris pile up. Eventually, the net breaks because of the weight of the debris. Then the net can no longer catch any fish.

The second fisherman takes out the fish and the debris. But he doesn't repair the net, and eventually holes develop that let some of the fish through. Each year he catches fewer and fewer fish.

The third fisherman takes out the debris along with the fish, so that the debris doesn't pile up. But he also repairs the net, and even adds to the net. Each year he catches more and more fish.

Think of the fish as the benefits of marriage, the debris as annoying habits, and the net as habits that meet marital needs.

Bad marriage partners are like the first fisherman. Annoying habits accumulate over time, and the weight of all these habits ruins the willingness to meet marital needs. Eventually there are no longer any benefits of marriage.

Mediocre spouses are like the second fisherman. Annoying habits are eliminated. But no new habits to meet marital needs are developed, and some of the habits that did meet these needs are forgotten. Over time, the benefits of marriage erode.

Good marriage partners are like the third fisherman. Annoying habits are eliminated; forgotten habits that once met marital needs are restored; new habits that meet marital needs are developed. Year after year the benefits of marriage increase.

In marriage, *compatibility is created*. As a couple increase the number of habits that meet each other's marital needs, they improve their compatibility.

This concept is very simple, but completely overlooked by most couples. You can only go one of two ways: You can let nature take its course and lose compatibility over the years; or you can *decide to become compatible* by making sure that you're meeting each other's marital needs.

We have an opportunity in marriage to give each other exactly what we need. So many couples squander that opportunity. Don't let it happen to you!

Six
The Fourth Insurance Policy—
Time

The older I become, the more I value time. There is simply not enough of it. It's been true all my life, but now there's more to do, and less time to do it.

We're tempted to cut the time allotted for each of life's objectives, so that more can be packed in. But some things take as much time as they ever did. Shortening the time wrecks the outcome. For example, marriage is wrecked when not enough time is taken to meet marital needs.

Before Sharon and Mike were married they spent the majority of their free time together. Her girlfriends knew that spending time with Mike was one of her highest priorities. Whenever they would invite her somewhere, she would first check to see if she'd be missing an opportunity to be with Mike. Her girlfriends thought it was silly. On some occasions she even broke dates with her girlfriends if Mike had time to be with her.

Mike did the same. Soon he found that many of the things he enjoyed doing were abandoned because he was spending so much time with Sharon.

They would try to see each other on a daily basis. On days that they couldn't get together, they called each other and sometimes talked for hours.

The total amount of time spent with each other in an average week was fifteen to twenty-five hours. This included time on the telephone. But they weren't counting. They took whatever opportunities there were, and it turned out that way. And when they were together, they tended to give each other quite a bit of attention.

After they were married, however, a change took place in the quality of their time together. While they were with each other much more often, they actually spent less time giving each other attention. Mike came home and watched television all evening; sometimes he barely said a word to Sharon.

Before they were married, they scheduled time to be with each other. But after marriage, they felt that "dates" were not as important, so their time together became incidental to other priorities in their lives.

How to Achieve Honesty, Protection, and Care

Courtship is a custom that gives people a chance to prove they can meet each other's marital needs. If enough love units are deposited, marriage usually follows. Honesty is tested; protection is tested; care is tested. But without time, none of these factors that create the feeling of romantic love is possible. And without time, romantic love cannot be sustained. That's why my fourth policy is essential to a complete and fulfilling marriage.

> ## Time
> ---
> **Give your undivided attention to your spouse**
> **a minimum of fifteen hours each week,**
> **meeting some of your spouse's**
> **most important marital needs.**

The three parts of this rule help me explain how it is to be applied in marriage:

1. *Privacy:* The time you plan to be together should not include children, relatives, or friends. Establish privacy so that you are able to give each other undivided attention.
2. *Objectives:* During this time, review and practice the policies of Honesty, Protection, and Care. Create activities that will meet some of the most important marital needs: Affection, sexual fulfillment, conversation, and recreational companionship.
3. *Amount:* Choose a number of hours that reflects the quality of your marriage. If your marriage is satisfying to you and your spouse, plan fifteen hours. But if you suffer marital dissatisfaction, plan as many as thirty hours each week or more, until marital satisfaction is achieved. Keep a permanent record of your time together.

One difficult aspect of marriage counseling is scheduling time for it. The counselor must work evenings and weekends because most couples will not give up work to make their appointments. Then he must schedule around a host of evening and weekend activities that take the husband and wife in opposite directions.

Another difficult aspect of marriage counseling is arranging time for the couple to be together to carry out their first assignment. They think that a counselor will solve their problems with a weekly conversation in his office. It doesn't occur to them that it's what they do after they leave the office that saves their marriage. And to accomplish anything they must reserve time.

It's incredible how many couples have tried to talk me out of this rule. They begin by trying to convince me that it's impossible. Then they go on to the argument that it's impractical. Then they try to show me that it's impractical for *them*. But in the end, they usually agree that without time their marriage cannot possibly survive.

Let's take a look at each of the three parts of this rule.

1. Privacy

The time you plan to be together should not include children, relatives, or friends. Establish privacy so that you are able to give each other undivided attention.

Why be alone?

Because when you're alone as a couple, you have an opportunity to deposit more love units in each other's Love Bank. When you're with others, everyone gets a little credit, but when you're alone *all* the credit goes to each other's accounts. Besides, without privacy, romance in marriage simply comes to a halt. And when that happens, love units start to escape from the Love Bank.

First, I recommend that couples learn to be without their children for a few hours each week. I'm amazed at how difficult an assignment that is for some people. They don't regard their children as company. To them, an evening with their children is *privacy*. They think that all it prevents is love-making, and they can do that after the children go to bed. But it prevents much more than that: It keeps them from focusing attention on each other, something desperately needed in marriage.

Second, I recommend that they learn not to include friends and relatives when they go out together. Only after they have accumulated enough time alone in a week may they include others. In many cases, there's no time left over. Again, the reason I make this recommendation is to encourage romance.

Third, I teach couples what giving undivided attention means. Remember, it's what you did when you were dating. There's no way you would have married if you had ignored each other on dates. You looked at each other when you were talking, you were interested in the conversation, and there was little to distract you. You must do the same things now.

When you see a movie, the time watching doesn't count because you're not giving each other undivided attention. Television is the same. So are sporting events. I want you to engage in these recreational activities, but the time that I'm talking about is to be very clearly defined: It's the time you pay close attention to each other.

Now that you're alone with each other, what should you do with this time? The second part of this rule helps me explain the answer to that question.

2.   Objectives

During this time, review and practice the policies of Honesty, Protection, and Care. Create activities that will meet some of the most important marital needs: Affection, sexual fulfillment, conversation, and recreational companionship.

The three policies I've already introduced—honesty, protection, and care—cannot be accomplished without reserving time to be alone.

Honesty requires time alone to explain feelings, personal history, daily activities, and future plans. Without time alone you'll never do it. Protection also requires time alone. Many violations of the protection policy come when there's been no time to negotiate. Demands are seen as short-cuts. "We have no time to argue; just do what I say!"

Care most certainly requires time alone. Some of the most important marital needs cannot be met unless you give each other undivided attention. The need for romance (affection, sex, conversation, and recreation) is met when you're alone.

Romance for most men is sex and recreation; for women it's affection and conversation. When all four come together, men and women alike call it romance. That makes these categories

somewhat inseparable. My advice is to combine them all, if you
can, whenever you're alone with each other. That's what people
do when they are having an affair. Why limit romance to
affairs?

Now for the final part of this rule. How *much* time do you
need?

3.   Amount

**Choose a number of hours that reflects the quality of your
marriage. If your marriage is satisfying to you and your spouse,
plan fifteen hours. But if you suffer marital dissatisfaction, plan
as many as thirty hours each week or more, until marital
satisfaction is achieved. Keep a permanent record of your time
together.**

How much time do you need to sustain romance? It depends
on the health of a marriage. If a couple is deeply in love with one
another and find that their marital needs are being met, I have
found that about fifteen hours each week of undivided attention
is usually enough to help insure a romantic marriage. It is
probably the least amount of time possible.

When a marriage is this healthy, it's either a new marriage, or
the couple have already been spending fifteen hours a week alone
with each other. When I apply the fifteen-hour principle to new
marriages, I usually recommend that the time be evenly distrib-
uted through the week, two to three hours each day. When time
must be bunched up, all hours on the weekend, good results are
not as predictable. People seem to need intimacy almost on a
daily basis.

For couples on the verge of divorce or entangled in an affair,
I recommend a much accelerated program. In such cases I have
often advised couples to take a leave of absence from work and
other responsibilities, go on a vacation to be alone, and spend the
entire time restoring the intimacy that has been lost over the

years. In many cases, two or three weeks of undivided attention to each other will bring a couple to a point where they can consider remaining married. I'm usually counseling them long-distance during this time.

The vacation alone cannot usually build enough love units to recreate the feeling of love. But the feeling of hatred is reduced and sometimes eliminated. Remember, in bad marriages, love unit balances are in the *red*. Negative accounts must first be brought to zero before positive accounts are built. These vacations are designed to speed up the love unit deposits.

When marriages are unhealthy but not on the verge of divorce, I recommend an intermediate amount of time alone together, somewhere between twenty and thirty hours each week. Without the crisis of divorce at hand, I usually have great difficulty talking people into being alone this long.

It has always been a mystery to me how workaholic businessmen find time to have an affair. The man who can't be home for dinner is scheduling mid-afternoon adventures three times a week. How does he get his work done? The answer, of course, is that he had the time all along. It was simply a matter of priorities. He could just as easily have taken time to be with his wife. Then he would have been madly in love with her instead of his secretary.

The reason I have so much difficulty getting some couples to spend time together is that they're not in love. Their relationship doesn't do anything for them, and the time spent together seems a total waste. But it's with that time that they can learn to re-create the romantic experiences that first brought them together in a love relationship. Without that time, they have little hope of restoring the love they once had for each other.

Whether your marriage needs fifteen hours a week or more than that, remember that the time spent is only equivalent to a part-time job. It isn't time you don't have, it's time you've filled with something less important.

Charting Your Marital Stock

To help couples get into the habit of scheduling time alone, I have encouraged them to make a chart, measuring the number of hours alone each week. Each person independently estimates the time actually spent giving undivided attention, and the number on the chart should be the lower of the two estimates.

This graph becomes an excellent predictor of marital fulfill-ment. It's like the Dow Jones Average of marital health. During periods when a couple spends large numbers of hours alone together, they can look forward in future months to a very warm and intimate love relationship. But when the chart shows that very few hours have been spent together, in the months ahead the couple can expect to find themselves arguing more often and feeling less fulfilled in their marriage.

I also encourage a husband and wife to carry an appointment book with them. In this book they write down the time they've set aside to be with each other. While I'm counseling them, I make certain that they keep the dates they set for each other, and that they are always recorded.

The total amount of time you spend together doesn't neces-sarily affect the way you feel about each other in the week that the time was spent. It has more effect on the way you're *going to feel* about each other in future weeks. It takes the Love Bank a while to build up before you start feeling its effects. But you'll be building love units, if you practice honesty, protection, and care. And the time you spend alone with each other will be among the most fulfilling and valuable moments of your week.

Applying the Four Policies to Common Marital Problems

Now that my four policies for successful marriage have been introduced, I'd like to teach you how to use them to solve your marital problems.

Since there are literally thousands of problems, I'll pick eight of the most common to show you how to apply these rules. You should then be able to use them to solve any of your own problems.

The first five problems are relatively easy to solve. While they're all capable of ruining a marriage, the application of my four policies is fairly obvious and effective. These problems are conflicts over 1) friends and relatives, 2) career choices, 3) financial planning, 4) child-rearing, and 5) sexual interest. Then, applying my four principles, we'll tackle some of the more difficult marital problems: 1) drug and alcohol addiction, 2) infidelity, and 3) emotional disorders.

When you've read these chapters, you'll be ready to apply my four policies to your own marital problems. And you'll find that they work!

Putting the Four Policies to Work

Seven
How to Keep
Friends and Relatives
From Destroying Your Marriage

David knew that Karen was attached to her family while he dated her. In fact, some of their dates turned out to be evenings with the Mitchells, even when they had other things planned. But on the whole they spent quite a bit of time alone, at least enough time to fall in love. The Mitchells were a conservative Minnesota family, and David enjoyed their company very much.

After their marriage, however, Karen was insistent upon seeing her parents whenever they had free time. At first David went along with it because he thought it was some symptom of separation anxiety. But after two years it became wearing.

"Karen, why do we always have to do everything with your parents?" David finally asked. "We're over there every weekend and almost every evening. I think it's about time we develop friends outside of our families."

"I thought you loved my parents!" Karen shot back. "Did they do something to offend you?"

"No, no, no," David said quickly. "I *do* love your parents. It's just that they're monopolizing our time. We're not developing friends outside our families and we're not spending much time alone."

Karen was unsettled. "Well, I can't think of better friends than my parents. Maybe you don't even *like* them."

"I said I *love* them," David objected. "But they're monopolizing our time. We need to break away from them."

Karen burst into tears. The subject was not brought up again until she discovered she was pregnant. The first person she told was her mother. In fact, David did not hear about it until he came home from work to find that she was over at her parents' house. Then he became angry. "Why didn't you call *me* first? It's *our* baby, not your mother's!"

Karen had no reply.

Now David was becoming alarmed. He could see himself being swallowed into her family. He even began to look for a job in another state.

After their first child was born, the situation was worse. Karen's parents would visit regularly—unannounced—and privacy was almost nonexistent. David complained once in a while, but Karen insisted on preserving her dependence.

One day David came home with an announcement. "I have exciting news! I've been offered a management position with a new company. They'll increase my salary, and we'll have a company car."

As Karen was rushing to the telephone to call her mother, he added, "We'll have to move to Dallas."

Karen stopped dead in her tracks. "We can't move to Dallas! It's too far from here. I wouldn't be able to see my mom and dad!"

By now, Karen was aware that she was too dependent on her parents, but she couldn't bear the thought of being without them.

David had already realized that if he didn't do something soon, her parents would wreck their marriage. He stood his ground.

"My career is important to us both. I can't lose this opportunity. Either you come with me or I'll have to go alone."

As it turned out, they did move to Dallas. While the adjustment was difficult at first, it resolved their most serious marital problem. From that point on, they were able to develop many new friends. More importantly, they learned to create and value privacy in their marriage.

In this illustration, Karen had violated two of my policies for successful marriage: protection and time. (You may need to go back to chapters 4 and 6 to reacquaint yourself with these policies.)

The policy of protection was broken when David expressed his annoyance with Karen's habit of seeing her parents so regularly and her unwillingness to change the habit. Her habit was causing her to gain at his expense. As soon as David told her that he objected to the time she spent with her parents, she should have stopped seeing them so often.

When she demanded that they spend free time visiting her parents she was again gaining at his expense. And she was not protecting him from her own selfish desires.

The policy governing time was broken because she would not schedule time to be alone with David. The experiences of intimacy essential to a healthy marriage were written out of her schedule.

In a way, David made a mistake by taking matters into his own hands and moving to Dallas. He violated the policy of honesty by failing to explain to Karen what he was planning. He told her that he was moving to further his career, when in fact he was trying to get her away from her parents. He also violated the policy of protection by *demanding* that they move to Dallas.

It worked out in their case because, once in Dallas, Karen's habits of dependence were broken and love units stopped draining out of her account in David's Love Bank. She was able to follow the policy of protection in Dallas whereas before it had seemed impossible.

They were also able to follow the policy of time because they developed the habit of giving each other undivided attention— well over fifteen hours each week.

But David could have been just as successful if he had

explained the plan from the beginning and given Karen a choice. Instead, he manipulated her. In general, manipulation fails to achieve marital objectives and usually causes lasting resentment. To this day Karen complains about how he forced her to move to Dallas.

Remember, my four policies apply to each spouse separately. If either spouse violates a policy, the marriage will usually suffer. *But you should never violate a policy yourself to resolve a problem created by a policy being violated by your spouse.* If Karen had never overcome her dependence on her parents, the marriage may have ended in divorce. She would have continued to lose love units in David's Love Bank until there were none left. But he chose a solution that risked the loss of his love units in her Love Bank. There were solutions available that would not have risked her love for him, and he should have tried those first.

Conflicts Caused by Friends and Relatives

In my years of counseling experience, I have witnessed a wide variety of marriages crippled and sometimes destroyed by relatives and friends. Let me describe just a few of the ways that this happens:

1. *Marrying into a dictatorship.* There are many would-be tyrants out there posing as parents. They controlled their children with an iron rod, and you happened to marry one of their children. Now that parent is still trying to control your spouse's life—and your life besides.
2. *Trying to be a friend to a former lover.* Some people actually believe that there's nothing wrong with continuing a "friendship" with a former lover after marriage. In every case I've ever seen, it hasn't worked out!
3. *Selling everything and giving it to the poor.* Bill was astonished to find how many poor friends and relatives Judy knew. Since their wedding, they began to surface,

first with requests for small loans, then with demands for help to avoid starvation. Judy was generous with them all—at Bill's expense.

4. *Your people shall be my people.* When a couple marries later in life (over thirty), a common problem can develop: They may come into the marriage with some very close friends that are disliked by their spouse. These are not former lovers but simply good friends they have known for years. While some friends of one spouse quickly become friends of the other, those who do not become a source of serious marital conflict.

5. *What's a little infatuation among friends?* Another common marital problem is the opposite of the last one: You come to like your spouse's friend *too much!* Tom fell in love with his wife's best friend, Emma. And then went on to have an affair. What a mess!

There are hundreds of marital problems caused by friends and relatives. I've selected only a few for consideration, but I believe all of them can be analyzed and resolved by applying my four policies. Let's see how they apply to the five problems I've listed.

Parental Tyranny

Many parents make the sad mistake of not letting go. But when parents are in the habit of dictating their child's every move, their effect on the subsequent marriage is usually devastating.

Shortly after marriage, Ellen told John that in order to keep peace in her family he must join the Lutheran church. Having been a Baptist all his life, he preferred continuing to attend his church, which he and Ellen had been attending before their wedding. After serious discussion, they decided to attend the church of their choice, the Baptist church. When told of that decision, Ellen's parents announced that they would not speak to either of them until they changed their minds.

At first Ellen was tempted to obey her parents, at John's expense. But in the end, she was mature enough to understand that his feelings had priority over her parents'. They decided to honor her parents' request for silence. It took two years, but her parents finally broke silence and admitted they'd made a mistake.

For some couples, parents have broken the relationship permanently. But in the worst instances, the parents have succeeded in dominating the marriage, with disastrous results.

The only reason parents gain the upper hand in their children's marriage is that a habit has been formed *giving them that upper hand*. Parental control should cease once you're an adult, but it's sometimes difficult to assert yourself after your parents worked so hard to teach you obedience as a child.

I am a firm believer in honoring one's parents: Obedience is an entirely different matter. Children should obey their parents because parents are usually much smarter than their children. But once children are grown, the parents' advantage disappears, and their offspring are able to make decisions for themselves. To continue demanding obedience often reflects an unreasonable need for control.

The most important reason that married couples should not obey either set of parents is that such obedience usually breaks the policy of protection in some way. Ellen was faced with the choice between obeying her parents and demanding that John join the Lutheran church, or disobeying her parents and making no demands. She enjoyed attending the Baptist church, so John's attendance was not bothering *her* at all.

By following the policy of protection, Ellen strengthened her marriage at the risk of weakening her relationship with her parents. She had her priorities straight! Her decision guarded her love units in John's Love Bank.

Friend and Former Lover

When Sue asked Jack (her new husband) to have dinner with Sam (her former lover), Jack was dumbfounded.

"Have dinner with Sam? Are you crazy? He's the last person in the world I'd even want to see, let alone have dinner with," Jack complained.

But Sue's persistence paid off—for her. Jack reluctantly agreed to dine with Sam and Sue. She simply wanted to maintain a friendship with Sam and didn't want it to be behind Jack's back. Doesn't that make sense?

I asked Sue, "Why would you put your husband through such an unpleasant experience? Didn't you realize how hard it was on him?"

"Oh, sure," she replied. "But I thought he'd eventually get used to it and the three of us could always remain friends."

Jack didn't get used to it, and it became the single most damaging event of their marriage. He never did get over it. It seems obvious that a former lover wouldn't be welcome in a marriage. I've never seen a case where it's been a good idea to maintain a friendship with a former lover. Yet many people try to maintain these friendships even when it's obviously hard on their spouse.

Sue wanted to continue her habit of seeing Sam. That habit annoyed Jack considerably, but she felt it was her right to see whomever she pleased. She violated the policy of protection and the resulting loss of love units was disastrous to their marriage. Jack was so hurt by her failure to protect him that he began violating policies, too. He violated all four of them. He was dishonest, critical and rude, did little to meet her marital needs, and wouldn't spend any time with her. This caused him to lose love units in her Love Bank. By the time they came to see me, they hated each other. Both of their Love Bank accounts were overdrawn. But over a two-year period, enough love units were restored that they could develop love for each other on their own.

First, Sue came to understand how much she had hurt Jack. She not only apologized but learned to overcome several other annoying habits. Then Jack had to go to work to straighten out his own behavior. It was a long and difficult process for both of them, a process that could have been avoided if they had protected each other from the beginning.

Welfare Directors

Judy had always been generous. That's one of the traits that attracted Bill to her. But after their marriage he began to feel drained by her generosity. While she had never earned much money, he had—and that's one of the traits that attracted her to him.

"We cannot support your sister and brother-in-law, Judy. He'll have to find a job, just like everyone else," Jack declared.

"But he's tried, and if we don't help, who will? Please, Bill," she begged, "let's help them just one more time."

They did help. But it wasn't just that time, it was many times thereafter. Eventually Judy's sister and brother-in-law moved into their house—and remained for five years. Both couples had a child during that time, and that put an even greater strain on the situation.

Even though I'm in the business of social service, I have been wary of handouts. I've seen many people become dependent on charity who would have become self-sufficient if the charity had not existed. I'm in favor, however, of professional counseling that motivates people to become self-sufficient. My colleagues and I have donated thousands of free hours of counseling toward that end. But Judy and Bill were not professional counselors, and what they gave her sister and brother-in-law did not help them in the end. It only made them dependent.

But what's much worse, Judy violated the policy of protection. And in doing so she lost valuable love units in Bill's Love Bank.

When is it wrong to be generous? It's wrong when you impose the cost of your generosity on your spouse. It's one thing for both of you to agree to be generous, but it's quite another thing for one of you to be generous at the expense of the other.

Judy felt good giving to her sister, so she gave whenever she had an opportunity. But as soon as Bill found out, he was furious. They had trouble paying their own bills, and when she gave away his monthly earnings, she was putting Bill under needless financial pressure. Her habit of generosity annoyed him, and since she did nothing to break the habit, she violated the policy of protecting him from herself.

When Judy insisted on inviting her sister and brother-in-law to live with them, she violated the policy of protection in another way—forcing her demands on Bill. She also violated the policy of time. Bill came home one day to find them ready to move in. While she did ask if it was okay with him, she didn't give him the choice of "no" for an answer. She had not protected his feelings, and love units poured out of her account. Since it was also an invasion of their privacy, they had an extremely difficult time arranging any time alone.

Again and again Bill tried to talk Judy into asking them to leave, but she was resolute. "I can't do that to my sister. You'll have to understand."

Bill may have understood, but Judy's love units in his Love Bank kept drifting away until there were none left to withdraw. At that point he became sarcastic and unkind. Even though it meant leaving his child, whom he loved dearly, he could no longer tolerate the conditions that marriage forced upon him.

Bill's leaving brought them to me for counseling. I was able to persuade Judy to reconsider her generosity to her sister. First she came to realize that her own child was suffering from the effects of her generosity. Then, and more importantly, she acknowledged that Bill had been suffering. Before Bill returned home, Judy made the commitment that she would never again try to impose her sense of generosity on Bill, even if she thought he was wrong. With the obstacle of her generosity gone, the marriage was very successful from that point on, since they both had so much to offer each other.

Sharing Friends

Craig and Joan could not understand how to get around the problem. He knew that there was really nothing wrong with her friend, Bev. But he was annoyed with her. In fact he was annoyed whenever Joan talked to Bev on the telephone.

They came to me for counseling because Joan thought Craig was crazy. "Maybe I could straighten him out," she said, "and then he'd be normal and like Bev."

He wasn't crazy. He just didn't like Bev.

Every one of us knows one or more people whom we dislike. I can't believe that Will Rogers wasn't annoyed by *someone!* It's normal to like some people and dislike others. Furthermore, just because you love your spouse there's no guarantee you will like your spouse's friends.

Most of us who are married notice that the friends we had before marriage are not the same as those after marriage. Look at your wedding pictures. How many of those people do you still regard as close friends? For most of us, only those who were friends to *both* spouses before marriage remain friends after marriage.

Friendships are more difficult to develop than most people realize. And they depend on individual taste. In general, there is nothing wrong with people I don't like, and there is nothing wonderful about people I do like. It seems that I'm programmed for certain people and not for others. Most people find this to be true for them as well.

Joan was inconsiderate of Craig's feelings when she insisted on continuing her relationship with Bev, knowing that it annoyed him. Joan wanted to think that being annoyed by Bev constituted mental illness. She didn't realize that she was violating the policy of protection. And in doing so, love units were pouring out of her account in his Love Bank.

After convincing Joan that Craig wasn't crazy and that she now needed to choose friends that they both liked, she eventually eased out of her relationship with Bev. They have since formed new friendships, and Joan is just as happy with her new friends as she was with Bev.

It was a matter of priorities. Joan decided that Craig's feelings were more important than her friendship with Bev, and that solved their problem. Love units were no longer withdrawn, and their accounts started to grow again.

Too Much Love

When Tom retired, he and his wife, Alice, bought a mobile home in a resort community. They liked the area so much they encouraged their best friends, George and Emma, to buy the home that was for sale next door to them. It turned out to be a great idea until George died.

After his death, the three of them remained very good friends. Tom was more than willing to help Emma with repairs, and he often went over just to keep her company. Within a few months he had fallen in love with her. He didn't tell Alice that he was in love with Emma, but he did tell Emma. She was also in love with him. Before long he was doing more than keeping her company!

This went on for over a year before Alice caught them. They were both ashamed and begged her forgiveness, but she could not be consoled.

Do you forgive your friend's offenses and continue the relationship? Or do you abandon the relationship forever?

This problem affects married couples of all ages. It is particularly troublesome among retired couples who have been life-long friends. I know of more than twenty cases where the offending spouse was over seventy years of age. It's remarkable, yet predictable. Why *wouldn't* you fall in love with a life-long friend?

This problem is a violation of all four marital policies. In fact, an affair is usually impossible unless all policies are broken by one or the other spouse.

Tom's most critical mistake was violating the policy of honesty. First, he failed to tell Alice that he had fallen in love with Emma, then he kept his love-making a secret. Tom had many excuses why he kept the truth from Alice: He didn't want to hurt her feelings; he knew how important Emma's friendship was to Alice; it was a short-term fling that would end soon with no one the wiser. But none of these excuses was adequate. He had been dishonest. He had broken the policy of honesty, and the result was a near marital disaster. Without honesty, solutions to marital problems are impossible, because information critical to a solution is distorted.

Tom also violated the second policy—protection. He developed a habit that was good for him but bad for Alice. He gained at her expense. His "habit," the affair, inflicted unbearable pain on Alice once it was uncovered. He did not protect her from his own selfish behavior.

It was Alice who broke the third policy—care. Tom had complained all their married life that their sexual relationship was inadequate for him. He never dreamed he'd have an affair, but when Emma told him how much she fantasized having sex with him, he found her irresistible. His sexual need had created a vacuum, and once it was filled by Emma he was hooked. If that need had been met by Alice, he would have had a much easier time resisting Emma's advances.

Tom and Alice both violated the fourth policy—time. Even though they were retired and had all the privacy they could need, they spent very little time giving each other their undivided attention. When they were together, he would sit and read and she would knit and watch television. On the other hand, the conversations that Tom had with Emma were romantic, they expressed deep feelings, and they certainly gave her his undivided attention. He spent *more* than fifteen hours each week with Emma, following the fourth policy, but it was with the wrong woman. It wasn't that Tom and Alice *couldn't* do it, but rather, that they *didn't* do it. It left them both vulnerable to an affair.

Even though there was considerable damage done to each other's Love Bank accounts by violating these policies, the accounts were ultimately restored.

When they came to me for counseling, the first thing I did was to teach Tom the importance of honesty. Over the next few weeks, he told Alice everything. She was terribly upset by his revelations, but she recovered. He promised her that he would never lie to her about anything again, even if it was something that would hurt her feelings.

We then designed a plan to break Tom's habit of seeing Emma. Tom and Alice sold their mobile home and moved to another retirement community in another state. The move was hard on both of them, but it prevented him from being tempted to see Emma, and it kept Alice from worrying about them seeing each other behind her back. Tom was willing to make the move, even though he was still in love with Emma. He knew that he could not trust himself. When the move was complete, he had restored compliance with the second policy—protection.

For the first time in their marriage, Alice took their sexual relationship seriously. At sixty-eight, she had rarely experienced sexual arousal and didn't think at her age it would be possible. But within a few months, she learned not only how to be sexually aroused but how to climax while making love to Tom. That experience created a sexual need that she had never felt before. She was employing the third policy, care, because she learned how to meet Tom's need for sexual fulfillment.

Finally, Tom and Alice learned to give each other their undivided attention at least fifteen hours each week. They restored romance to their marriage and, while it was a painful process, the outcome was something that neither of them believed possible. Their only regret was that they had not followed the four policies throughout their married life, preventing the disaster that almost ruined their lives.

*   *   *

Marital problems involving friends and relatives are overcome when couples keep my four policies for successful marriage. Friends and relatives don't always like the solutions, but the marriage is always left in great shape.

The problems are usually created when the policy of protection is violated. Your friends and relatives cannot impose themselves on your spouse unless you let them. It's *your* behavior that you must control to protect your spouse. When you cater to your friends or relatives at your spouse's expense, you are violating the rule of protection, and love units are lost. Your spouse is your most important friend and relative. No other friend or relative should ever come between you.

Eight

How to Keep
Career Choices
From Destroying Your Marriage

Moving is never easy—but it's excruciatingly painful when you don't *want* to move. Jean was in tears all day long as she packed.

"Ed, Duluth may be a wonderful city, with wonderful opportunities, but I like it here in Sioux Falls. Please, don't do this to me," she begged.

"I'm sorry," he replied, shaking his head, "but we can't turn back now. I was fortunate to be offered this job and I can't pass it up."

Jean did move to Duluth with Ed. Then she moved to Des Moines, Kansas City, and finally Minneapolis. They invested thousands of dollars in her therapy during his travels. Their children had not been in one school for any two-year period of time and were starting to have trouble adjusting socially.

I was Jean's next therapist in what was already a long list. She was anxious, depressed, angry—all classic stress symptoms. The methods already used to treat her were, for the most part, standard fare. But nothing had worked.

My first impression was that her marriage was terrible, but sometimes it's difficult to know if a bad marriage causes emotional symptoms or vice versa. She absolutely hated Ed. She made love to him regularly but felt that it was like making love to a pig in a barnyard. I tentatively concluded that it was the marriage that caused the symptoms and asked to see her husband.

Ed loved Jean dearly, tried to put her first in everything, valued his time with his family, and was intelligent and attractive besides. He seemed to be every woman's best choice for a husband. What could have been the source of Jean's hatred toward him?

All signs pointed to the move from Sioux Falls. Jean brought it up constantly, and whenever she was most depressed she reported that she had no hope of ever going back "home."

I explained to Ed that his wife could take drugs all her life to counteract the effects of all his moving around, or he could go back to Sioux Falls, and within two to five years she'd be back to normal. Even if I was wrong, it was worth a try because she was so neurotic that her treatment was becoming prohibitively expensive and painful for the whole family.

Ed was able to get an excellent job in Sioux Falls, and the last I heard, they and their children were doing great.

This case illustrates a major point: *You* know what you need better than anyone else. Jean knew she would suffer if she moved away from Sioux Falls. And she did suffer. But short of a divorce there was no way to return home.

Jean experienced a conflict that commonly causes severe emotional symptoms: If she were to choose moving from one strange community to the next she would suffer; and if she were to choose a divorce she would suffer. This type of conflict is often referred to as an Avoidance-Avoidance Conflict. In other words, it makes no difference what you do, you will experience pain. Conflicts like this tend to make people neurotic.

If Ed had followed my second policy for successful marriage, protection, none of this pain would have resulted. Ed's gain was at Jean's expense. He thought that he knew what Jean needed, but his mistake cost her years of unhappiness and caused his account in her Love Bank to go bankrupt.

When Ed finally did follow the rule of protection, two things happened at the same time. First, Jean felt much better and was "cured" of her emotional disorder; second, the depletion of love units ceased, and his care for her started building back his Love Bank account.

My wife, Joyce, and I experienced a similar situation, but we handled it differently. I was offered a wonderful career opportunity in Chicago (at least it was for me at the time), but Joyce was not happy about moving from beautiful Santa Barbara. We came to an agreement: She was willing to go, on the condition that we could move back if she didn't adjust well, and we would live in a neighborhood of her choosing. I never demanded that we move; it came through negotiated agreement.

We then moved from Chicago to Minneapolis, again through negotiation, and my daughter, Jennifer, was placed in four different schools that year. Then Joyce's father died. It was a time of great emotional upheaval in her life. But through it all she knew that, if she wanted, I'd be willing to move back to Santa Barbara.

As it turned out, she loves the Twin Cities, and she has been very happy living there. It would now be much more difficult for *me* to negotiate a new move!

Conflicts Caused by Career Choices

The examples in this chapter are selected to give you a taste of how career choices can destroy a marriage. In each case, the problem was avoidable, but because of ignorance the choice created needless pain and suffering. There are many other examples I could choose, but these will be enough to help you avoid the same types of mistakes in your marriage.

1. *Being addicted to work.* I think we've all been acquainted with a workaholic. But what is it like being married to

one? From the cases I've seen, there are advantages and
disadvantages. But mostly disadvantages!

2. *Driving your life away*. Careers that take you away from
your family for days at a time—such as trucking, air
travel, sales, and armed services—are hazardous to your
marital health. If it were not for these careers, marriage
counselors, such as myself, might starve.

3. *Marrying Saint Francis*. When one of you catches the
vision to become a minister or missionary and the other
doesn't catch the same vision, is one of you a saint and
the other a sinner? If so, sometimes it's hard to know
which is which.

These three problems were created through failure to subscribe
to one more of my four policies. But their resolutions are possible
when the same four policies are properly applied. In each case,
try to guess which policy was violated and how it was violated.

The Workaholic

Your career should always serve your marriage. Your marriage
should never serve your career. Unless, of course, you're willing
to sacrifice your marriage for your career. The workaholic is a
good example of someone who has his career out of perspective.

I've worked a great deal with folks in nursing homes and have
talked to many people who are close to death. I've *never*
encountered someone who told me that if he had one regret, it
was that he should have spent more time at work. The regret is
often that he should have spent more time with his wife and
children.

Most of us want our spouse to be ambitious. But ambition, like
everything else, can get out of hand.

Renee didn't know exactly what she wanted in a husband, but
she knew one thing: She didn't want to marry a lazy oaf! So when
Jim came along, she was very impressed with his tireless ability to
work. He not only put himself through college, but saved enough
to pay cash for his car. It made her feel secure to know that he was
not the type to pile up debts.

While Jim and Renee were dating, he saw her or called her every day. Being with her was a part of his schedule. But after they were married, his career took off and his time with Renee crash-landed.

"Jim, you're working too hard," she would tell him. "Why don't you relax a little? Let's take a vacation together."

He would just smile. "I am relaxed! Have you ever seen me on a vacation? I'm a bundle of nerves."

Jim didn't realize, and Renee didn't explain, that the problem was not his nerves but their relationship. They were not with each other often enough to sustain romance. The relationship had become boring to Renee.

Renee came to me to express her dissatisfaction. She lived in a beautiful home, had wonderful children, and all the freedom a mother could ever dream of. But she lacked romance. In fact, she was seriously considering an affair just to see if it would help.

A first mistake was Renee's violation of the policy regarding honesty. She had not explained to Jim that she was unhappy with their relationship, because she thought it would make her seem unappreciative of all the material things he provided. And she didn't dare tell him she was thinking of having an affair. He might leave her and then where would she be?

The most critical mistake, however, was Jim and Renee's violation of the time policy. They both enjoyed each other's company and knew how to meet each other's needs, but without time there was no opportunity.

Getting Jim to see me for an appointment was a Herculean task. He was scheduled for months ahead, so I adjusted my schedule to fit his. Even then, he would cancel at the last minute if a business emergency arose. My message was simple: Either take fifteen hours every week to be alone with your wife, or prepare for marital disaster.

I explained that Jim's failure to take time to be with Renee ruined every opportunity to meet her marital needs. His financial support was far beyond anything she needed, and he was committed to his work at the expense of meeting all other marital needs. If he loved Renee and cared about her, he should at least listen to her explain the problem.

When I finally had them together, she did a great job of honestly explaining her feelings. At first he thought I'd brainwashed her. Eventually she convinced him that they had been her true feelings all along, but she had been afraid to express them.

I convinced Jim to take a four-day vacation alone with Renee that very week. That followed with Renee filling twenty-five hours of his next week. They spent twenty hours alone together the third week, and by the fourth week, they were together fifteen hours. Everything else fell into place. They learned to express themselves honestly, they protected each other, and they met each other's most important marital needs.

Jim is still a workaholic, but Renee has his undivided attention fifteen hours each week and romance has returned to their marriage.

The Traveler

Without a doubt, I can thank the airline industry for giving me the opportunity to make a living as a marriage counselor. Their employees helped me become an expert on the subject of infidelity, because many of these folks were having affairs. They also gave me confidence in my methods, since they proved successful even in these cases!

Any career that takes you away from your spouse overnight is dangerous to the health of your marriage. The more you're gone, the more dangerous it is.

Sarah absolutely loved her job as a flight attendant. She liked the work itself, earned a very good salary, and could travel almost anywhere as an employee benefit. Her husband, Rich, didn't like her job at all. She had applied for the job without consulting him, knowing he wouldn't like the idea and thinking that she probably wouldn't get it anyway. But when the job was actually offered it to her, she was delirious with excitement.

When Rich came in the door from work, Sarah flung her arms around his neck. "I got it! I got it!"

He smiled and hugged her back. "Got what?"

"I got a job as a flight attendant. Isn't that great! Oh, I'm so happy!"

Rich's smile faded. But Sarah didn't notice. She ran all around their apartment screaming, "I got it!"

"Hey, wait a minute, Sarah, you didn't tell me you were applying for a new job. Don't you like the job you already have?"

"It was okay, but I never thought that I'd be able to work as a flight attendant. It's okay with you, isn't it?"

Rich finally yielded. "Well, I guess we can try it for a while to see how it works, but I'm not too crazy about having all those men gawking at you all day long."

Six months later, the job was becoming a major issue in their marriage. Rich was left alone for up to three nights at a time and was becoming more and more jealous. Sarah would come home to find a beast in her apartment; by the time he settled down she was off on another trip.

When Rich and Sarah came for counseling, Sarah was not sure she was in love with Rich anymore, because he had become so abusive. And she thought she might be falling in love with someone she met on a flight. She suggested that a separation might be a good idea, so she could decide how she felt about her marriage.

Rich didn't know about any of this and simply wanted me to tell her to quit her job.

I'm a practical man. Sarah was hanging onto the marriage by a thread. I couldn't *tell* her anything and have her show up for the next appointment! So I had to start with Rich. I explained that, for a while anyway, he would have to tolerate her job while restoring her interest in the marriage (building love units).

Rich had been violating the policy of protection by being

abusive and demanding that Sarah quit her job. This had drained all the love units from his account in her Love Bank. She simply didn't love him anymore.

I was able to convince Rich that it was in *his* best interest to control his abuse of her and to stop making demands. In return, Sarah agreed not to separate while in counseling. His success in keeping the protection policy was probably the most crucial step toward their recovery.

Then I was able to help Sarah overcome her first mistake — dishonesty. With Rich's commitment to protect her, she was able to explain her feelings to him and even went so far as to tell him that she was thinking of moving out, that she might be in love with someone else, and that she didn't love him. By that time, his love units had started to accumulate in her Love Bank. Within a few weeks, she was comfortable living with him and was not afraid to express her feelings. Then I explained to her that she had violated the policy of protection. When she took her job, she gained at his expense.

Her face turned red. "Well, I suppose you want me to quit my job. That's what you really want, isn't it?"

I explained that she could do anything she wanted. I had no right to demand anything of her and neither did anyone else. But the policy of protection would help insure the success of her marriage. Without it her marriage would probably fail. Any marriage would probably fail.

Sarah did quit her job, and they both learned that they couldn't afford to gain at each other's expense. Eventually, she found another job in the airline business that gave her many of the same benefits yet didn't take her away from her husband nights.

Before we go to the next example, I might add that changing careers sometimes leads to catastrophic economic consequences. A truck driver, for example, can't always just quit his job and find something else. A manufacturer's representative may have spent ten years building his accounts and can't just walk away from them. Quitting a job isn't always necessary. What is necessary is that you have ample time to give each other undivided attention every week and that whatever you agree to do satisfies you both. If you can work out a compromise where, in all honesty, you are both happy, then it's a good solution.

Another point that I should make is that being on *different work shifts* is also a marriage killer. Let's say you work first shift and your spouse works second shift. That leaves you eight hours to either be together awake or together asleep. In most marriages it's a show stopper! You become like ships passing in the night.

Another marriage killer is *rotating shifts*. I've seen many clients suffer from depression while on these shifts only to overcome the symptoms when they switch to a single shift. Not only do rotating shifts wreck emotional stability, but they tend to leave marriages in shambles because good marital habits become almost impossible to sustain. It's much easier to develop good habits if your daily schedule is repetitive.

The Saint

Your career should always serve your marriage. Your marriage should never serve your career. Those who use their marriage to serve their career often lose their marriage. This can even happen to well-intentioned religious people who are motivated by a desire to serve God and help others.

Al committed his life to the ministry when he was nine. He went forward at a church service when the preacher asked for a commitment from those willing to become full-time ministers. Al never forgot that commitment. In college, he majored in Bible to prepare for the ministry.

Toni was also a Bible major and had thought of becoming a missionary. They took many of the same classes and studied together. They dated, and before long, they were in love.

Before they graduated, Toni decided against becoming a missionary, changed her major to social work, and eventually

completed that major. Al figured that social work would be a
great background for a minister's wife and encouraged her in her
professional training. What he didn't realize was that Toni had
decided against being involved in *any* full-time ministry. Toni
knew that Al was thinking of being a minister but didn't think
about how it would affect her. She thought it would probably be
the same as any other career, and she didn't have to be involved
in it.

Al and Toni were married immediately after college gradua-
tion. He enrolled in seminary and she found a job as a social
worker. After one year of seminary, they both came to grips with
the fact that she was not willing to be a part of his ministry.

"Toni, I can't be a minister unless you're as committed as I
am. You have a very important role to play as a minister's wife,"
he explained. Then he trotted out Bible verses on the subject of
a man's authority over his wife.

Toni became furious. "Don't lecture me. I'll do what I please,
and if I don't want to play Mrs. Reverend, I won't."

Then they broke into the biggest fight they'd ever had. When
it was over, Toni agreed to support him in his ministry. But she
didn't like it at all.

After Al graduated from seminary, they took a position in a
rural church with fifty members. Al was very happy with his
career, but Toni suffered. She could not fit the role that was
expected of her. There was little privacy in the church parsonage,
and she hated living in a fishbowl. She put on a cheerful face
when she met parishioners, but when she was home alone, she
cried. Al felt that her problems were spiritual and that she had
not given herself to God's work. Her "rebellious spirit" was
keeping her from enjoying the ministry as much as he enjoyed it.
She believed him!

Toni's depression became so bad that she could no longer hide
it from others, and eventually Al felt she should see a psychologist.

It didn't take me long to find the problem. Toni explained that she was not cut out for the role of pastor's wife. She had come to hate her husband, yet she could not divorce him because it would not be God's will and it would probably ruin Al's ministry.

Al had violated the policy of protection. He imposed his career on her even though he knew she was suffering. He demanded that she perform duties to further his ministry, even though they made her uncomfortable.

The policy of protection forbids the imposition of anything that causes suffering, even if you feel you are morally justified. In Al's case, he felt that he had the authority of the Bible to defend his behavior, but the consequences were marital disaster. His failure to protect Toni caused such a great loss of his love units in her Love Bank that eventually he was severely overdrawn. She hated him. What's even worse, she was on the brink of suicide.

Even though Al's behavior didn't show it, he cared a great deal for Toni and came to realize that her depression could not possibly be in God's will. Nowhere in the Bible could he find support for forcing his career upon her. Over a period of months he agreed to go back to school and study to become a counselor. Toni took a job as a social worker to support him, and I saw her recover completely from her depression.

Al has now completed his retraining and has a job as a psychologist. The last I heard, Toni was in love again. He works closely with churches and supports ministers in their pastoral counseling.

It is all a matter of priorities. In Al's case, he had to realize that once he was married, *Toni had to be his highest priority*. His marriage could not serve his career. His career had to serve his marriage, especially when his career was serving God.

*   *   *

When my four policies for successful marriage are kept, career choices are not made unilaterally. Both a husband's and wife's careers are chosen with each other in mind. Furthermore, if a career *becomes* incompatible with either husband or wife, the career must be abandoned or modified.

Careers are not only chosen but *carried out* with consideration for both husband and wife. Even when I am in a counseling session, my wife can always interrupt, because she's more important to me than my career.

My career was planned with my wife in mind. In fact she ruled out my first three career choices before we could agree. It sure makes sense, doesn't it? Don't let your career come between you and your spouse.

Nine

How to Keep
Financial Planning
From Destroying Your Marriage

Frank didn't seem to worry much about his finances. He earned enough to get by and that was always good enough for him. He never borrowed money.

After high school Frank moved from his home into a mortuary where he worked (while he slept) as night attendant. He earned free meals at his part-time job as waiter and took the bus whenever he needed transportation. Grants paid his way through college, and he managed to complete his education without borrowing a dime.

Ellen realized that Frank couldn't afford much while he was attending college and admired his financial discipline and resourcefulness. Although their dates and his gifts to her were inexpensive, they were thoughtful and reflected his deep love for her.

But after Ellen and Frank were married and were both earning a good income, financial conflicts began to develop. Frank insisted from the beginning that all their income go into a bank account that only he controlled. Ellen knew that he was a good money manager and he wasn't squandering their income—but he wouldn't tell her how the money was being spent. It didn't bother her until she started to think about raising a family.

One day she posed an important question. "Frank, do you think we're ready to raise children?"

"Not yet," he replied. "It'll be a while before we can afford them."

Ellen bristled. "We can afford children now! We both earn a good income and we've been saving most of it—haven't we?" Suddenly she felt uncomfortable. "By the way, how much have we saved?"

There was a long pause. "We just haven't saved enough. Take my word for it," Frank said.

That got Ellen's curiosity going. The next day she was home alone, she started poking through Frank's papers. What she found amazed her. Frank had all of their investments in *his* name—savings accounts, money market accounts, stocks. And the most remarkable part of it was that he had managed to save over $25,000 in just two years!

That evening Ellen confronted him with her discovery.

"Why are all our savings in your name? And how can you say we can't afford children when we've saved $25,000?"

Frank was furious. "I handle all the finances, and I do it the way I see fit. Besides, you wouldn't understand it even if I tried to explain it to you. So stay out of my desk!"

Frank might have been *saving* money, but he was *losing* love units. Ellen was terribly offended and decided to end the conversation.

The very next day Ellen opened her own checking account. When she was paid, she deposited her check into it.

That evening, Frank said casually, "You haven't given me your check. Do you have it yet?"

"Yes, I do," she said flatly, "and you're not getting it."

This time *she* lost love units in *his* Love Bank. In fact, for the next year, she lost love units each time she deposited her check into her own account. It seemed fair to her, but he thought she was being selfish.

By the time Frank and Ellen saw me for marriage counseling,

their complaint was that they had "grown apart." She had her life, and he had his. Their inability to resolve their financial conflict had implications in many other areas of their lives; their separate checking accounts had begun the process of separating everything.

Their problems began with Frank's violation of honesty. He had not told Ellen what he was doing with their money and why he was doing it. He was keeping more from her than just financial information: He was hiding important information about his thoughts and his behavior. With incomplete information, Ellen gradually suspected Frank of trying to cheat her.

Frank's motives were pure: He was saving money for both of them and was not trying to cheat her. But his arrogant approach destroyed her trust in him.

Ellen also violated honesty when she set up her own checking account. Even though Frank had not been honest with her, she should have been honest with him. If she had followed the policy of honesty before deciding to have a separate checking account, she would have told him what she was planning to do and why.

Then they both violated the policy of protection. When Ellen explained that her discovery of their savings in Frank's name had upset her, he refused to transfer their investments into joint accounts. He knew that his actions had been at her expense but did nothing to protect her from them. If he had followed the policy of protection, he would have added her name to all the investments and would not have demanded that she deposit her check into his account.

Ellen also violated the policy of protection when she opened a checking account and deposited her checks into it. Even though most of us would consider her actions reasonable, they were a violation of the policy because they offended Frank. If she had followed the policy, nothing would have been done with her checks until she had come to an agreement with Frank. Frank could not have forced her to deposit those checks in his account or *he* would have violated the same principle of protection.

To stop the drain of love units from their Love Banks, I

explained to them that they had to start employing the policies of honesty and protection.

It didn't take long for Frank to agree that he shouldn't have kept his investment strategy to himself, even though he felt it was in Ellen's best interest. Putting investments in his name was for convenience, and he had no intention of cheating her. He was offended that she didn't trust him. But he came to realize that she had a *right* to the information he had kept from her—she had a *right* to claim his honesty.

Both Frank and Ellen agreed that from that point on all financial decisions would be made together, all investments would be made in both of their names and their paychecks would be deposited into a *joint* checking account. When it came time to pay the bills and decide how much would go to savings, they would come to an agreement before any checks were written.

Frank and Ellen went on to have children and, as far as I know, they're still following my policies for marriage, building love units along the way!

Conflicts Caused by Financial Planning

I have struggled with many couples over the issue of financial planning. I explain to them that it's a choice of love or money: Which is their *first* choice?

If they choose love, then they shouldn't ever make financial decisions at the expense of their love for each other. When couples make this choice, they should earn and spend money with consideration for each other. With that condition they usually end up with love *and* money!

If they choose money, then they shouldn't gain love at the expense of their money. When couples make this choice, they usually lose their love for each other and, more often than not, their money as well.

When the policies of honesty, protection, care, and time are followed, money is never earned or spent at the expense of love.

These policies do nothing more than keep love a higher priority than anything else. Love is what holds marriages together, not money. When couples forget that fact, they squander their most valuable possession, love.

I've chosen three cases that help me apply my policies for successful marriage to conflicts in financial planning.

1. *Puttin' on the Ritz*. If your spouse spends like there's no tomorrow, you'll both pay when tomorrow finally arrives. Keeping your spouse out of financial trouble is a losing game. The rules of the game must be rewritten if love units are to be won.
2. *Driving together down the road to bankruptcy*. If you and your spouse find yourselves headed for insolvency, you may lose something far more valuable than your money: You may lose love units. But there's a way to experience financial disaster without experiencing marital disaster.
3. *It's all a matter of priorities*. Your basic values are often reflected in where you spend your time and money. Since most couples don't share exactly the same values, those differences usually come out in the budgeting of time and money. What do you do when you can't seem to agree on financial priorities?

In my book, *His Needs, Her Needs*, I devoted a chapter to making realistic budgets and learning how to stick to them. If you need help in budgeting your money, I encourage you to read that chapter. But in this chapter, I'll skip some of the details of budget-making and devote time to the more general issue of learning how to make financial decisions with mutual consideration.

The three illustrations that follow show how to apply my four policies to financial planning in marriage.

The Spendthrift

For many of us, spending more money than we have seems to be instinctive. We usually know that at least one of our ancestors was financially undisciplined. We must have inherited the trait from him!

Shirley had inherited the trait in its purest form. From early childhood she could not resist buying things that she wanted. Her father had tried to help her control her spending, but she became so upset whenever she couldn't have something that he would finally give in and hand her the money she needed.

While Sam dated Shirley, he'd buy her things that she wanted as gifts because he enjoyed seeing her reaction: She seemed to live for her next gift from him. Shirley was a very attractive woman, and Sam's generosity brought the very best out of her; it made her appear even more attractive to him. Within six months they were both head over heels in love.

Since Sam was an executive in a growing company, he earned a very good living. But it never occurred to him that Shirley could cost him more than he earned. In the first few years of their marriage he justified many of her purchases as necessary for their new home. But she wasn't satisfied with her initial purchases and had to buy replacement items. The closets in their home were soon so filled with her clothes that she gave away many items to make room for a new wardrobe.

Sam became alarmed. "Shirley, I think it's time we discuss something. You're spending more than we can afford."

She became genuinely concerned. "Oh, Sam, are you having financial problems?"

"*We* are having financial problems! My income is better than ever, but you're spending more than I earn," Sam complained. "We'll have to start a budget so we can keep our expenses under control."

"That's okay with me," she responded cheerfully. "Just give me an allowance each month, and I'll stick to it!"

Sam worked out a budget for Shirley, but in the first month she *didn't* stick to it. When Sam tried to talk to her about it, she shrugged it off as a bad month and promised to do better the next month. But the next month was no better.

Now Sam became upset. "Shirley, are you trying to ruin me? You're spending money I don't have."

Shirley's voice remained calm. "Take it easy, Sam. You must be upset about something that happened at work. I think you're overreacting."

Sam couldn't hold his anger in any longer. "Overreacting? My problem is that I haven't reacted soon enough. I've got to put an end to this immediately. I'm taking your name off our checking account and canceling all our credit cards. I'm sorry, but it's the only way I can get your irresponsible spending under control!"

Shirley was visibly hurt by his words. She knew her spending was out of control, but she felt he had no right to treat her as a child.

The next time Shirley saw something she wanted to buy, she simply withdrew money from their savings account. Within six months, all of their savings were gone.

By the time Sam and Shirley came to my office, Sam was threatening divorce. "How can she say she loves me—and steal me blind? I just can't go on like this."

"I admit I have a problem controlling my spending, but I love Sam and I think he still loves me. He knew I liked to shop before we were married. I'm no different now than I was then," she said in her defense.

The honesty and protection policies were violated in this marriage. While Shirley was the major offender, Sam was not off the hook.

Shirley had a habit of buying whatever she pleased long before marriage, but it didn't cost her love units because her father paid. The gifts she had received from Sam represented a fraction of his discretionary expenses, and he enjoyed her reactions.

But after marriage, she didn't wait for him to buy her things. With checkbook and credit cards in hand, she could buy what she wanted without his permission, and that's what cost her love units. She broke the rules of honesty by failing to explain how she planned to spend their money (it was often impulse spending, anyway). Then she wouldn't tell Sam how much she'd spent and what it was for. He would discover her purchases only when the bills arrived.

After Sam informed her that her spending upset him, Shirley broke the policy of protection by failing to follow through on an agreement that would have accommodated his feelings. Her excuse that she had a "problem controlling her spending" was nothing more than acknowledgment that she was gaining at Sam's expense. She knew that he would be infuriated when he discovered their savings gone, but she cared more about buying that next item than protecting Sam's feelings. She lost love units in the transaction.

It is important to stop here for a moment and reflect on the fact that Shirley really did love Sam. She didn't spend their money to get even with him for some offense of the past. She simply neglected to protect his feelings, and in the process Sam lost much of his love for Shirley. This scenario is seen time and time again by marriage counselors.

In the process of counseling Shirley and Sam, I was able to convince him that she loved him as much as ever. But that knowledge didn't restore any of his love units. He simply didn't feel the love he once had.

In his effort to overcome the problem, Sam had also violated the protection policy. When he "told" her that she would not be able to use the checking account or the credit cards he made a demand. That tactic cost him love units and it did nothing to resolve the problem. He was on the right track when he tried to negotiate a solution, but when the initial effort failed, he should have gone back to negotiation, perhaps with the help of a marriage counselor.

Even though Sam's love was significantly reduced, he went ahead with a plan to restore love units. Shirley agreed to a strategy that helped her overcome her buying habits. She and Sam designed a budget, and she learned to live within it.

Although she had setbacks during the first few months, she eventually overcame the problem.

Shirley came to realize that every time she spent money without mutual agreement it was just like hitting Sam with a two-by-four. She was hurting him with that particular habit and, if it continued, his love for her would eventually disappear. So she learned to overcome the habit. In the process, Sam's love for her was restored. They came away from the experience with love and a more mature relationship.

The Conspirators

Financial problems are at the core of many divorces. They have a lot to do with the way people treat each other when financial disaster looms around the corner.

Mel and Edith where a happy-go-lucky couple who never missed an opportunity for a good time. Mel had a decent job but didn't earn nearly enough to support their standard of living. Edith worked when she felt like it, which wasn't very often. Most of the time, they got along very well. But whenever they had a conflict over money, sparks would fly.

Mel had a terrible problem with his self-esteem and, once in a while, Edith would remind him that Wilber, a former boyfriend, was earning more money. To prove to Edith that she had made the right choice, Mel would give her whatever she wanted—whether they could afford it or not. From time to time he would explain to Edith how seriously indebted they were, but it would invariably start a fight during which she blamed him for failing to earn more.

A point was finally reached where Mel could no longer pay his bills and, without telling Edith, he tried desperately to consolidate them one more time. He believed right up to the end that someone would lend him the necessary money. But one day the sheriff came to his home to serve his wife with a foreclosure notice.

Edith had a few guests over the morning that the sheriff arrived. She was embarrassed beyond words. When Mel came home that evening, he received the tongue-lashing of the century. Within a week she kicked him out of the house.

"When you have all this straightened out, you can return home. But until then I don't even want to look at you. You disgust me!"

"Listen to me for just one minute," Mel pleaded. "If it weren't for your reckless spending we wouldn't be in this mess. I've done the best I can to keep us from bankruptcy, and you just keep spending money like it's water."

"Don't make excuses for your laziness!" she fired back. "If you had an ounce of ambition we'd have plenty of money. Get yourself in gear or say good-bye."

Mel came to my office to see if I could help him save his marriage. I suspected that they'd played a game of deception with each other, and Edith probably didn't want to lose Mel anymore than he wanted to lose her. I arranged for an appointment with her and discovered I was right: She loved him as much as he loved her.

Neither of them was taking responsibility for their financial woes, however. And yet they were both to blame. In a way, they had conspired with each other to create the appearance of wealth. Their motives were different, but they both knew what they were doing. They just weren't willing to accept the inevitable consequences. Many of these situations end in divorce because, at this point, both husband and wife become vicious in an effort to shift blame to the other. They punish each other so effectively that it's not long before one or both of their Love Bank accounts is overdrawn and the marriage comes to an end.

But I was able to catch Mel and Edith before too many love units had been lost. I explained to them that the policies of honesty and protection had been violated in their marriage. Even though Edith would become upset whenever Mel discussed finances with her, Mel broke the policy of honesty by failing to regularly inform her of their financial condition and what he was doing to try to improve it. She wouldn't have been surprised by the sheriff if he had been honest with her.

Edith violated the policy of honesty by failing to tell Mel that the reason she'd become so upset when they discussed money was that it made her feel guilty. So she'd blame him, trying to shift the guilt. It was a game that worked for the short run, but almost led to divorce.

The policy of protection was violated every time they had a fight. Because they tried to blame each other for their problems and then punish each other, love units were lost quickly whenever a discussion of their finances turned into an argument.

Mel and Edith did lose their house and had to file for bankruptcy. But their marriage remained strong because they both accepted partial blame for what had happened to them. In a way, it gave their marriage a new start that it couldn't have had without a clean financial slate.

With this new start, they learned to share financial information with each other and to make decisions together. Before long they were in a home they could afford and their standard of living kept pace with their income.

I'm almost certain that Mel and Edith will have financial problems again in the future. Almost all married couples do. But when these problems develop, they won't be using the solutions of the past that lost love units. Instead, they'll use solutions that build love units!

The Idealists

Those who have tried to mediate between a husband and wife often find that both have legitimate positions. But sometimes their positions are poles apart. Helping them decide on a compromise sometimes takes the wisdom of Solomon.

The issue that divided Henry and Marsha was how to budget their income. Henry had a good job, but he was always afraid he'd be laid off and the family would have nothing to fall back on. Marsha was more confident of Henry's job security and felt that helping their children pay for college was more important than savings. Saving part of each paycheck for unforeseen emergencies was a good idea. But helping their children through college was also a good idea. Which of the two was the better?

Marsha and Henry came to my office in the hope that I would decide the issue for them. The solution to their problem, of course, was not mine to choose. They had to decide for themselves. But I explained how my four policies would help them.

To begin, I explained that whatever they decided had to strengthen their love for each other. Their highest ideal must be the building of marital love. They had never quite thought in those terms, but it didn't take them long to agree with me. I also pointed out that ideals are often in conflict, and that it's important to establish the priorities of your ideals. Financial planning is an opportunity to set your priorities—but don't forget to set your love for each other as the highest priority.

Then I had them explain to each other why their position was important to them. Henry told Marsha about his fear of losing his job and having difficulty finding another. Having a savings account that would carry them for a year would make him feel much more secure, since he felt that he could be re-employed within a year. She felt that the savings would be a waste since he was already investing in a retirement plan, and the main purpose of a padded savings account would simply be to provide him with an added sense of comfort.

Then Marsha expressed her concern that without financial assistance their children might miss the opportunity to complete a college education. She considered it the obligation of parents to see their children through college. Since Henry had never attended college he wasn't so sure that college was a necessary step toward adulthood.

They had both passed the test of honesty, and now they were ready to consider protection. To pass that test, the outcome could not annoy either of them. I explained that one solution that passed the test of protection was to neither save their money nor help their children. (Remember, you have to *do* something annoying to violate the policy. Doing *nothing* may also be annoying but, technically, it doesn't violate the policy of protection). They both objected to that solution and immediately set out to come to a compromise.

"How would you feel if . . ," took the place of, "Stop being so stubborn!" Marsha suggested that she work more and that her salary go to their children's education. When she asked how Henry felt about that idea, he pointed out to her that it would take her time away from him and that if they gave the children money for college, he wanted it to come from both of them.

Henry suggested that he wouldn't object to cosigning student loans. If they had the money later on, they would pay off the loans for their children. When she was asked how she felt about that idea, Marsha explained that she didn't want her children to face life with debts, even if there was the possibility that they would be paid later.

Through their discussion of possibilities, they learned not to challenge each other's feelings. Even when they seemed unreasonable, the feelings were accepted as final. This created for both of them a much greater willingness to cooperate. They became more and more creative in the discussion and finally arrived at a solution that they both liked.

When their negotiations were over, Henry and Marsha agreed that the most important outcome of discussion was the love that they felt for each other. In fact, it got to a point where both had reversed their original positions: He was willing to sacrifice his savings for the children's education and she was willing to use the money for his savings.

The ultimate compromise was a combination of taking some money from savings (but not enough to make Henry uncomfortable) and cosigning a student loan that Marsha did not feel would be too burdensome. But the compromise built love units, and that was the most important outcome.

                              *   *   *

In each of these cases, financial planning came between a husband and wife. What should have been to their mutual advantage, ended up to their mutual disadvantage and they lost love units in the transaction.

The policies most violated were honesty and protection. This is typical for problems in financial planning. There are a host of marriages in which one spouse is in the dark concerning the family finances. The other spouse, the one who is usually best with numbers, pays the bills and determines the budget. This condition violates the policy of honesty, even in cases where the other spouse seems to show no interest in family finances.

The protection policy is violated when budgets are created to benefit one spouse at the expense of the other; or when money is spent by one spouse without the approval of the other. The policy is also violated when, in an effort to gain financial control, one spouse makes financial demands on the other.

Whenever these policies are violated, love units are lost. It's that simple. But if financial planning takes my four policies into account, couples succeed in achieving the highest objective of marriage: love.

Ten

How to Keep
Children
From Destroying Your Marriage

Raising your own children is difficult enough. But raising someone else's children can require the patience of Job. When patience is in short supply, love units are at risk. Careful planning is needed to avoid disaster.

Greg was a single parent with two teenagers, Allan, thirteen, and Vivian, fifteen. The three had a comfortable lifestyle, and he tended to spoil his children. Since the death of his wife eight years earlier, Greg had dated only two women, Bobbi and Janet. He liked them both very much, but Janet enjoyed being with his children and Bobbi didn't. That single factor caused him to break up with Bobbi and eventually marry Janet.

As soon as they were married, however, conflict developed between Janet and Vivian. Once Janet had moved into their home, Vivian started "borrowing" her clothes without asking. Janet didn't say anything at first, but after her favorite sweater disappeared, she'd had it!

"Vi, have you seen my pink sweater?" she asked.

Vivian didn't miss a beat. "Nope."

"Are you sure?" Janet pressed. "You may have taken it to school and left it there."

"I've never taken any of your sweaters to school! Why would you think I took it?"

"Well, you've taken some of my other clothes, and I thought that maybe you'd taken the sweater too."

"I can't believe this! Look, I haven't taken your sweater. Okay?"

There was no way to prove that Vivian had worn the sweater, but Janet knew her clothes hadn't grown legs and walked off. When Greg came home that night she explained her problem to him. Then he asked Vivian about the sweater. She denied ever wearing it and became angry that they were ganging up on her over something she had nothing to do with.

After that incident, more of Janet's clothes disappeared. One day while Vivian was in school, Janet searched Vivian's room and found almost all of her missing clothes. When Greg came home she told him what she'd found. He confronted Vivian with the evidence. She burst into tears and denied having had any of those clothes in her room. It was her word against Janet's, and she accused Janet of lying. In an effort to calm everyone down, Greg said they'd discuss the matter some other time.

Janet was furious.

Vivian put a lock on her door.

As the months passed, the relationship between Janet and Vivian worsened. When her father was gone, Vivian made uncomplimentary remarks to Janet and openly challenged her right to live there. Greg tried to stay out of the growing conflict. But one day Janet could take no more.

"Greg, it's either me or Vivian. The two of us can't live in this house together."

Greg was stunned. "What do you want me to do? I can't kick out my own daughter. Besides, she'll only be with us for another three or four years. Can't you hold out that much longer?"

"Yes, Greg, I could. But I won't. It's perfectly clear to me that she comes first in this house—and I'm not living in a home run by a spoiled brat!"

"I think we have *two* spoiled brats living in this house," Greg countered, "but Vivian's only fifteen! What's your excuse?"

Janet moved out.

In my office, Greg and Janet reviewed the disastrous first year of their marriage. They both thought they'd made a mistake marrying each other.

I reminded them that prior to marriage, they were highly compatible and loved each other as much as they had loved anyone. Their loss of love was a direct result of the way they'd handled Vivian: She had come between them. They needed to discover a way to complete the job of raising her without destroying their love for each other.

During that first year of marriage, Greg had lost almost all his love units in Janet's Love Bank because she felt so bad living with him under those conditions. And she started treating Greg badly as a result, which caused her to lose love units in his Love Bank.

We agreed to try to restore those lost love units.

The policy of honesty had been violated because Greg had not explained to Janet what he was up against. In my office, he told her that he had never punished Vivian for anything. When he knew she had taken Janet's clothes, he didn't know how to respond. He tried to avoid the issue, but his avoidance turned out to be destructive: He left Janet with the impression that he didn't believe her and that he had no interest in helping her resolve the conflict.

Greg admitted to Janet that he'd known all along that his daughter had taken her clothes but didn't want to punish Vivian. I explained to him that it would have been quite helpful if he had made that clear at the onset. A solution could then be found that wouldn't require him to punish her.

The next step was to decide how to handle a situation in which Janet was being verbally abused. Simply telling Vivian to stop wouldn't work. We decided that the process should begin with

Greg agreeing to work with Janet toward a solution. They would discuss alternatives until they found one that was mutually agreeable.

The policy of protection was followed very carefully. They made no demands on each other and agreed that they would not settle on a plan that annoyed either of them.

The violation of the time policy had been another critical factor in their loss of love. Prior to marriage, they spent about twenty hours each week at Janet's apartment, or out on dates where they gave each other their attention. But after marriage, they were rarely alone with each other. The children were with them when they were at home, and they seldom went out.

To resolve the problem, Greg and Janet committed themselves to reserve twenty hours each week to be alone together. They would use some of that time to discuss the children and resolve issues created by child-rearing conflicts. They also agreed never to discuss these subjects in front of the children.

I recommended that Janet remain separated from Greg until the solution regarding Vivian's behavior was implemented. For several weeks they worked on this problem together and eventually agreed on a strategy to overcome it.

Janet admitted, of course, that the loss of her sweater was not as painful as the feeling of being abandoned by Greg. He admitted that he was in the habit of defending his daughter unconditionally, and it was clearly at Janet's expense. He agreed to consider her feelings first in family decisions, the same way he'd treated his first wife.

This was a significant turning point in their crisis. When Greg agreed that protecting Janet's feelings would be among his highest priorities, the crisis was essentially ended. That was all Janet wanted from him. She knew that teenage girls can be hard to handle. But she wanted reassurance that when Greg married her he'd put her first in his life.

With Janet gone for several weeks, Vivian started feeling guilty. On her own initiative, she invited Janet back to the home but never did admit stealing the sweater. Although she didn't take any more clothes from Janet, she was still rude and insulting.

The next time she offended Janet—and it was within a week of her homecoming—Greg and Janet discussed the problem with Vivian as if it affected them both. He explained to her that whenever she hurt Janet's feelings, she was hurting him too. She had to learn that her dad was now a part of Janet; if she loved him, she needed to care for his new wife. It took Vivian about a year to make that transition.

By teaching his children to be considerate of Janet's feelings, Greg implemented a very good child-rearing method, one that helped both children learn to become less self-centered. But something else was far more important: Greg and Janet learned that once they were married, not even his children should come between them. They also learned that privacy was what helped create their love and they needed privacy to sustain that love.

Conflicts Caused by Children

Even when the children are your own, they can easily come between you and your spouse. In your efforts to give *them* the best opportunities in life, *your spouse may suffer*.

When a conflict arises between a husband and wife over how their children are to be treated, marital priorities are sometimes overlooked. Children are too important to some parents: Therefore, a wife may give her husband the impression that the children are more important than he is, and vice versa. Problems of child-rearing are imposed on one spouse by the other in a way that leaves the one feeling neglected.

My four policies help keep child-rearing in perspective. I've selected three cases that help demonstrate how the four policies are applied to these conflicts.

1. *Marrying Mother Hen.* Kris was the *perfect wife* until her first child was born, and then all the attention she had been giving to Wayne was shifted to little Rachel. Three

children later, Wayne was certain that marrying the *perfect mother* had been the biggest mistake of his life.
2. *Squeezing three into a bed.* Most children want to sleep with their parents. But it can sure interfere with certain intimate experiences. Couples need to use other forms of birth control or love units will be squeezed out.
3. *Ruling with a mighty arm.* When does discipline turn into abuse? Children know, and usually the nonoffending parent also knows. It is less likely for children to suffer abuse when *both* parents can agree on methods of discipline. Without such agreement, love units also suffer abuse.

People usually enter marriage with the best intentions to be loving and caring *partners* in life. But when children arrive, a new ideal—to be loving and caring *parents*—sometimes conflicts with the ideal of partnership.

The policy most often violated in child-rearing conflicts is that of time. When children enter your life, they'll take away the time you gave each other prior to their arrival. You may not have realized that time was essential to your marital happiness until it is gone. But by then you may find yourself helpless to do anything about it.

Another policy commonly violated is protection. One parent makes up rules that are not agreed to by the other and punishes the child when these rules are broken. For many parents, such one-sided child-rearing is infuriating and often leads to massive Love Bank withdrawals.

The following three cases will help illustrate how common child-rearing practices violate these rules and lead to a loss of love.

The Super-Mom
Wayne had dated many women and was even engaged once, but no one seemed to meet his high standards well enough to make him want to tie the knot—until he met Kris. She was

everything he'd always hoped for, and she loved him too. She was absolutely perfect as far as Wayne was concerned.

Those who knew Kris well were not surprised by the good job she did as Wayne's new wife. She had a history of doing things well. Ever since early childhood, she was able to focus her attention on personal objectives and achieve them with excellence one by one. When she fell in love with Wayne, she wanted nothing more than to be everything he needed in a wife, and she was able to achieve it.

Kris became the perfect wife, meeting all of Wayne's known marital needs and some that he never knew he had. She was his lover, friend, recreational companion, and greatest admirer, and she kept herself extraordinarily attractive.

When Rachel, their first child, was born, Kris's focus of attention changed. Now she had a new personal objective: To be the perfect *mother*. At first, Wayne was delighted with the care and attention she gave their daughter. After all, he wanted the very best for Rachel and knew that Kris could provide it.

But after a while it became apparent that Rachel's gain was his loss. Kris couldn't leave Rachel for a moment, and when they were together as a family, Rachel had her mom's undivided attention. Wayne knew that somehow he had to find time alone with Kris.

Walking in the front door one evening, he said, "Hey, hon, let's go to the hockey game tomorrow night. A guy at work has tickets he'll give me."

"No thanks, not this time," she said pleasantly. "But you go ahead if you'd like, dear."

"What's gotten into you?" he teased. "You used to *love* the North Stars!"

Kris was not smiling. "We can't just have fun and forget about Rachel. She needs as much attention as we can give her. What we do for her now will affect the rest of her life."

"Now wait a minute! I'm talking about one evening out.

Surely her whole life won't be ruined if she spends an evening with your parents."

"I *said* I won't go. That's it!" Kris turned and walked out of the room.

Wayne wondered what had happened to his perfect wife. She must have left one day and her twin sister, the perfect mother, showed up in her place. He did go to the hockey game with a friend from the office. It started a pattern in which he worked late or went out with friends most evenings.

Even though their marriage was starting to deteriorate, Kris was insistent upon having more children. Over the next seven years, they had three more, and she dedicated herself to their care. They loved her dearly because she not only took responsibility for their training but was a cheerful, fun-loving mother.

She wished that Wayne would take a more active role in raising their children, but when she tried to discuss it with him he explained that with four children he had to work harder to keep up with the bills.

Wayne showed up in my office one day to try to gain perspective on his life. He was falling in love with a woman at work but didn't want to start an affair. Marrying Kris, he thought, had been the biggest mistake of his life. He couldn't go on living this way but didn't know how to change things without filing for divorce.

"All she really wanted was children. I don't think she ever really did want a husband," he told me. "I'm not even sure she loved me. How could I have been so stupid?"

I tried to assure Wayne that Kris had loved him and probably still did. She had simply made a choice between two ideals—being a good wife and being a good mother—and chose one at the expense of the other. She had not grasped the consequences of her shift in emphasis. At the end of our conversation, he was willing to let me speak with her about their marriage.

Kris was upset about the marriage too. She felt that he'd

abandoned her as soon as their children arrived. When he left her alone so much of the time it encouraged her to focus even more time on the children.

Over a period of weeks, I tried to persuade Kris that it was in the children's best interest for their parents to be in love. And she had to spend time alone with Wayne for their love to be restored. But she kept arguing that the solution to their problem was for Wayne to be home more often and for them to spend weekends together as a family. Then, she said, she'd have respect for him again. In short, I didn't get any farther with her than Wayne had. Finally, she refused to talk to me about it anymore.

At this point, Wayne was ready for a divorce. But I was able to talk him into waiting one more year, and during that year he had the sense to stay away from the woman who worked with him.

The first step toward recovery was a separation. Wayne explained to his wife that unless she would reserve time for him, he wouldn't return home to her. It put the ball in her court.

At first Kris was very angry and went to an attorney to file for a legal separation. But in about a week, she knew that what he was asking made sense and, without privacy, they had little hope of restoring romance to their marriage.

I recommended that, before Wayne return home, they take a week's vacation together. They had a lot of catching up to do. Kris also agreed to spend twenty hours a week alone with him for the first three months, and fifteen hours a week thereafter. (It's very important to do all the negotiating *during* the separation. Don't expect to gain too many concessions *after* returning home.)

It seemed like a miracle. During their vacation together the old Kris returned. Wayne couldn't believe it. But he noticed that as soon as she was home with the children, her twin arrived! How could that be? I explained that the children were bringing out the maternal instinct in her and that his hope for happiness was in holding her to the agreement to be alone with him each week.

That's exactly what he did. Today they're happily married.

Wayne now spends much more time with his family even though he spends fifteen hours alone with Kris. Where did all the time come from? It was there all along. As soon as Kris's priorities changed and they learned to keep the policy of time, everything fell into place. When they violated the time policy, none of the other rules could be acted upon. They couldn't care for each other (meet each other's marital needs), and they couldn't protect each other.

Time is a simple policy, but not one that is always easy to persuade people to follow. In the case of Wayne and Kris, it took a separation to motivate them.

Three's a Crowd

Greg and Patti had a great marriage, and when the kids came along it was still a great marriage. But there was one fly in the ointment: Susan, their three-year-old, insisted on sleeping with them at night. At first Greg thought it was cute. But after a while, when Susan became a nightly resident in their bed, he didn't think it was so cute anymore.

"Patti, we've got to do something about Susan sleeping with us," Greg suggested one morning over coffee. "Don't you think we need more privacy?"

"Oh, she'll outgrow it. It's just a phase she's going through," Patti responded.

"Well, it's starting to annoy me, and it sure has affected our love life!"

Patti shook her head. "If we tell her she can't sleep with us, she may think we don't love her. We can't do that. Just be patient."

The problem didn't improve for a solid year, and Greg became more and more upset. Before he had asked Patti to help him solve the problem, she hadn't lost too many love units in his Love Bank. But after she told him to just put up with it, he started to blame her for the problem—and love units were withdrawn at a rapid pace.

Every once in a while, he would raise the issue with Patti. Her response was always the same: She felt that it was wrong to create anxiety in Susan by forcing her to sleep in her own room. Besides, whenever they encouraged her to try it, Susan threw a fit.

Greg began to realize that he didn't love Patti as much as he once had and, in a moment of unabashed honesty, told her so. She made an appointment for counseling the very next day.

They both knew that Susan's bad habit of sleeping with them was an annoyance to Greg. But it never occurred to either of them that Greg's love would be affected by the situation. In fact, as he described possible causes for his lack of love, he blamed his work, personality flaws in himself, and negative attitudes toward women. Patti couldn't imagine what his problem was, since she still loved him very much.

After careful analysis, I guessed that Susan was the unwitting culprit and encouraged them to teach her to sleep in her own bed. Susan even came for one appointment so that I could explain to her how important it was to sleep by herself. She still raised a ruckus for a few days, but within a month she was sleeping soundly in her own room. I encouraged Greg and Patti to put a lock on their door in case Susan tried to sneak in at night (which she tried to do on several occasions). After a year they were able to remove the lock.

This whole procedure was very hard on Patti. She was afraid that Susan would be traumatized for life. But I reassured her that they were doing the right thing. If anything, Susan might grow up emotionally handicapped if they continued to encourage a habit that could lead to an unhealthy dependence.

An even more important consideration was that Patti had given her daughter a higher priority than her husband. As a result, the policies of protection, care, and time had been violated. Letting her daughter sleep with them annoyed Greg, and yet she did nothing to protect him from that annoyance. One of his most important marital needs, sexual fulfillment, was not being met, which violated the policy of care. The invasion of their bed also robbed them of some of the fifteen hours that they needed to be alone.

The plan worked. Once Susan was in her own room, Greg reported that his love for Patti was being restored. As soon as they solved that single problem all the great things they'd learned to do for each other took over, and love units poured in.

The Tyrant

Alex had a short fuse. Everyone in his family knew it, and his friends knew it. But when he fell in love with Christine, he knew that his temper would ruin his chances with her, and so he learned to control it. He also had the sense to know that he should never abuse her after marriage. So he vowed to himself— and to her—that he'd never try to punish her verbally or physically. So far, so good.

However, Alex was raised in a tradition where beating children was considered a parent's duty. As a child he'd been beaten. His parents had explained to him that he was to obey them or expect disastrous consequences. Since no one's perfect, he got the disastrous consequences from time to time.

When their first child arrived, Alex expected the same unwavering obedience that his parents had expected of him, and he beat his child the way he had been beaten. The first time it happened, Christine was very upset and begged him to stop.

The temper Alex had learned to control with Christine was now released on his children. Whenever he was irritated about something the children were punished more severely. They grew up with considerable fear of him. But all the while he was careful never to treat Christine abusively. In fact, he went out of his way to be sure she understood that his punishment of the children was a father's responsibility, something that had to be done.

All Alex's explanations never changed her feelings, however. Every time he beat their children, Chris suffered. It was as if he was beating her, and she cried whenever it happened. Even though he had shown exceptional care for her in other ways, the suffering of her children caused a huge loss of love units from his account in her Love Bank.

Alex was violating the policies of protection and care: protection because his behavior was offensive to Christine whenever he punished the children; and care because he was not meeting one of her most important marital needs, family commitment. Her need for family commitment implied that he would have a relationship with his children, not of fear but of love and respect; not abusive, but thoughtful and supportive.

Finally, after one of the children had been beaten for a trivial matter, she reached the end of her endurance.

"Alex, I can't take this anymore," she objected. "I don't care if the children disobey. Leave them alone! You're too hard on them."

"We've been through this before. Children will not obey their parents unless they are punished for disobedience. If I stop punishing them, I'll be encouraging them to sin."

"I don't care if they sin. Leave them alone!" she screamed.

Alex looked her right in the eye and said, "Christine, I'm sorry, but you'll have to submit to me, as you're commanded to in Scripture."

Christine saw me for counseling the next day, referred by her pastor. Apparently, none of her children had ever been seriously injured and there were no physician's reports that could have been used to support a case for child abuse. While the children had bruises from time to time, they never complained at school about beatings at home, and the teachers did not suspect abuse. It was one of those borderline cases in which I couldn't expect to use the courts for leverage.

So I had to try to influence Alex without the leverage of law. My appeal was simple. The punishment of his children was also punishment of his wife, Christine. She identified with them and suffered when they suffered. I explained that discipline should be a joint decision between husband and wife, if for no other reason than to preserve their love for each other. But I also pointed out that Christine had an important perspective on child-rearing that he should consider. A *joint* perspective would benefit their children greatly.

Fortunately, I had the support of his pastor. When Alex consulted with him about my advice, the pastor agreed with me and encouraged him to follow it.

Both Alex and Christine continued counseling with me to learn appropriate methods of discipline. To some extent, I let them settle on methods that Christine felt were fair. Alex was not too happy at first about a shift from punishment to a system of rewards to modify their behavior. But he soon discovered that rewards were far more effective in teaching his children good habits. Constant punishment merely created resentment and rebellion.

Alex had learned to apply the principles of protection and care to his marriage. He overcame a most annoying habit and developed a new one that met one of Christine's most important marital needs.

                              *   *   *

Children can come between a husband and wife, destroying the love that they have for each other. In most cases, it isn't the children's fault, but rather one or both parents who assign a higher priority to the care of their children than they do to the care of each other.

The policy most commonly violated is time. So much time is spent with the children that there is not time left to be alone with each other. Some parents feel that once children arrive, whenever they are with each other, their children should be included. I recommend that children be included *after* fifteen hours have been scheduled for privacy. For many families I've counseled, another fifteen hours is scheduled each week for family time, with children included. (See chapter 11, "Family Commitment," in *His Needs, Her Needs.*)

Other policies that are usually violated are protection and care. Protection, when methods of child-rearing are imposed without consideration of a spouse's feelings, and care when those methods fail to meet important marital needs.

When children come between a husband and wife, love units are lost. But when my four policies are followed, children are successfully integrated into a caring family without the loss of love.

Eleven

How to Keep
Sex
From Destroying Your Marriage

Alice was a very attractive woman. To be more precise, she was an absolute knock-out!

Fred was one of the few men she'd dated who didn't try to undress her on the first date. In fact the first date was spent discussing how to help the handicapped, one of her greatest concerns. Since they were both majoring in social work, they shared many of the same values. They spent hours discussing the problems of society, and he consistently expressed compassion for the underprivileged. He also had a profound respect for women and treated Alice with that respect.

Even though she had made love to some of her past boyfriends, Alice had felt guilty and sometimes used. When she explained these feelings to Fred, he suggested that they wait until marriage to make love. At first, she thought his suggestion was too impractical—but it got her attention and impressed her! She interpreted his patience as respect for her and a willingness to place her feelings above his selfish desires. He earned hundreds of love units for that "selfless" attitude.

After graduating from college they were married, and on their wedding night, Alice was looking forward to making love, having waited for two years. But Fred was too tired! Alice was crushed. She cried most of the night.

The next morning, however, they made love for the first time. Alice was visibly disappointed. He ejaculated after less than a minute of intercourse.

Alice wanted to try again that afternoon, but again, Fred was too tired. And, of course, that evening he was too tired. During their two-week honeymoon, they made love only five times, and each time it lasted only a few minutes. Alice must have tried to get him interested fifty times! It was a very frustrating start to their marriage, and she lost her temper. In fact, she threatened to get an annulment if he couldn't get his act together.

But Fred did everything else right. He was a great conversationalist. He was affectionate, considerate, and made her the center of his life. She couldn't have asked for anything more—except sex!

"What's the matter with you," she blurted out shortly after they arrived home.

"What do you mean?" he asked.

"Do you realize that when a girl is sexually rejected by her husband it makes her feel unattractive? Maybe I'm not your type!"

"Oh, no, Alice, you're the most beautiful woman I've ever seen."

With that Fred gave her a big hug, and made love to her. He made a real effort to improve their sexual relationship, but within three months he started losing his erection whenever they had intercourse.

"What does this mean, Fred? You really don't find me attractive, do you? All the time I thought you were treating me with respect, you were simply uninterested! Why did you marry me if you didn't find me sexually attractive?"

"You are sexually attractive, believe me. I simply have a

problem expressing it. I want to make love to you, but my body doesn't cooperate!"

"You're not telling me the truth," she pressed. "You must think I'm a fool! If I was attractive to you, your body would work just fine."

Neither of them wanted to see a counselor about sexual issues, so they tried reading every sex therapy manual they could get their hands on, but to no avail.

Finally Alice gave up. She loved Fred and that's what counted the most. But after six years of marriage, Alice started wanting an improved sexual relationship for a new reason: children. Fred rarely ejaculated during intercourse and, as a result, no children. They finally decided to see a counselor, not because of unfulfilled sexual need, but because they both wanted to raise a family.

What I discovered on my first interview was that Fred was more sexually frustrated than Alice. In fact, he had come very close to having an affair. On the other hand, she had resigned herself to a relatively sexless marriage and wasn't doing too badly. But he *needed* a good sexual relationship. And all the pressure she put on him had eroded her account in his Love Bank.

Fred sat in wonderment telling me how preposterous his situation was. Alice was, indeed, very attractive and most men would consider her the sexual fantasy of all time.

In almost all marriages, one spouse is more ignorant of his or her sexuality than the other. Usually it's the woman, but in Fred and Alice's marriage, it was Fred. He postponed sex until after marriage partly because of his moral principles. But it was also partly because of fear—he knew Alice was experienced, and he was not. He was afraid she wouldn't be satisfied with him. She intimidated him!

And when they first made love, all his worst fears were realized. He completely lost confidence in himself. By the time their honeymoon was over, he had been raked over the coals so many times that he had started to develop a strong fear of having sex with Alice. From there it was a short trip to impotence.

Fred violated the policy of honesty by not explaining to Alice what he was feeling. Even while dating, he should have told her that he was sexually inexperienced and afraid she would reject his fumbling attempts to make love. It would have given her an entirely different perspective during their honeymoon.

Honesty is incredibly essential to the development of sexual compatibility, particularly for the newly married. Alice had little to learn about her own sexuality, but she had a lot to learn about Fred's. And Fred had *much* to learn about his sexuality.

Alice violated the policy of protection in a major way. She ridiculed Fred's sexual performance because she thought he was being lazy and needed to be pushed. Besides, it made her very angry, and she felt better after she expressed her anger. She also demanded sexual performance. These violations not only kept Fred from overcoming his impotence, but caused also the loss of love units.

The assignment I gave them, a common approach to impotence, was to let Fred take the sexual initiative; Alice was to expect no sexual fulfillment for herself until their exercises were completed. He learned to maintain an erection without ejaculation for over ten minutes while having intercourse with Alice. He was also able to explain to her what she did to make sex unpleasant for him, and she made a few important changes in her method of lovemaking.

Alice had many sexual techniques in mind that had to be abandoned when they discussed the effects they had on Fred. She also wanted him to engage in sexual marathons from time to time (twenty-four hours of sex, nonstop), which appeared to Fred as torture. But by the time they had it all sorted out, they not only made love several times each week, but they both found it fulfilling.

Fred agreed to be completely honest with Alice about his feelings from that day on, and Alice agreed never to pressure him again. While no one is perfect, their three children are evidence that they've done a pretty good job!

Conflicts Caused by Sex

Fred and Alice had a serious sexual problem. When I first saw them, Fred had almost no interest in sex with Alice. And yet even minor sexual problems can wreak havoc in a marriage, because sex plays such a key role.

Years ago, as I was trying to improve my marriage counseling technique (almost every couple I counseled was getting divorced), I abandoned my emphasis on "communication" and switched to simply improving sex in marriage. I was an instant success! Today, I balance my emphasis across many marital needs but haven't forgotten that, without a good sexual relationship, a marriage is usually in serious trouble. And if you can get their sexual relationship on track, clients feel that the money they've spent for counseling has been well worth it.

The trick to solving sexual problems is to make certain that *sexual desires and behavior* do not come between a husband and wife. It's easier to see how children or a career can come between spouses, but sex can also be a very important agent of marital destruction, particularly when it is self-serving and not in the interest of *both* spouses.

My policies for marital success solve sexual problems. Sex, like everything else in marriage, must be mutually beneficial or it becomes a cause for the erosion of love units. I've chosen three cases to help me explain this to you.

1. *God's curse on women.* Some women think that sex is the way God punishes them for their sins. For these women, sex is painful enough to make them think it's a

punishment for something. But sinners and saints both experience *vaginismus*, and both can overcome the condition.

2. *What's everybody so excited about?* Almost one-fourth of all women go through life without experiencing a climax, not because they can't but because they haven't learned how! It's a delicate business, trying to teach women to climax, and husbands are sometimes particularly indelicate. But with sensitivity and knowledge, it's a sure thing.

3. *Sharing the experience.* Jealousy is common in marriage, particularly if a spouse finds another lover. But what do you do with a spouse that wants to make love to himself? Who's the target of your jealousy then? Masturbation in marriage has caused many love units to evaporate into thin air. Failure to share sexual experiences misses a great opportunity to build love.

Honesty is usually the first policy to be violated when sexual problems arise. Misunderstanding can be corrected only by the most honest expression of sexual attitudes and reactions to stimulation. Sex is often an area hidden from a spouse, which complicates and magnifies sexual differences that already exist. The solution to most sexual problems begins with unabashed honesty.

Protection is the second policy to be violated. Sex that benefits one spouse is often at the expense of the other spouse. Instead of mutual pleasure, it can take the form of rape. Sexual demands, which also break the policy of protection, are common in marriage.

Care is the third policy violated. Since sexual fulfillment is an important marital need, one of the most important marital skills is the ability to make love with sexual arousal and climax. It's easy enough to learn, but some people don't care enough about their spouses to go to the trouble. Whenever that happens, they've violated my third policy and an opportunity to build love units is lost.

Time is sometimes a factor in creating sexual problems. If you violate the policy of time, all the understanding and skill in the world will not create the opportunity to make love.

The cases I've chosen will help me explain to you how violation of these four policies helped create serious sexual problems that were solved by following them.

The Sinner

Evelyn was born out of wedlock, and her mother never did marry anyone. In fact, her mother had sex only once in her lifetime, and that was when Evelyn was conceived. That single sexual encounter had been extremely painful, and she was certain it was God's punishment for her indiscretion. She told her daughter that God often punishes women by making sex painful, and that if she ever married, she should expect pain while having intercourse.

Evelyn did marry, and her choice was Doug, a quiet, hard-working farmer. On their honeymoon her first sexual experience was as painful as she had ever imagined. In fact it brought her to tears. Doug didn't know what to make of it and figured that whatever it was, it would go away. He tried making love to her several times on their honeymoon and each time she ended up crying.

Remembering her mother's prediction, Evelyn simply expected to experience pain every time she made love. Over the next few weeks, the pain not only remained intense, but the opening to her vagina eventually closed each time intercourse was attempted. It became impossible for Doug to penetrate. Evelyn thought it was God's punishment for her mother's sin carried on to her. Doug thought it was her way of keeping him from having sex with her.

After the first few weeks of marriage, they attempted intercourse about once a year, but to no avail. On their fifth anniversary, he informed her that he was considering a divorce. That brought them to me for marriage counseling.

Both Doug and Evelyn incredibly naive about sex. Evelyn had been warned by her mother that God punishes sexual impropriety, so she had never engaged in any sexual experimentation. Doug had learned to masturbate but had no other sexual experiences prior to marriage. He felt that reading books on sex was a form of perversion. Coming to a counselor was clearly an act of desperation for both of them.

I assured them both that if they followed my instructions completely, their problems would be over within three months. It actually took less than six weeks.

Evelyn had a condition called *vaginismus*. It's a muscle spasm that closes the opening to the vagina. It's usually caused by tears in muscle tissue somewhere in the reproductive tract. It can also be caused by infection in the vagina. But it has nothing to do with sin.

I explained to Evelyn that her mother probably had the same condition when she made love her first and only time. Not knowing what to make of it, she passed it off as punishment.

I had Evelyn see a gynecologist first to be certain that she was free of infection and that she had a normal-sized vagina. Sometimes an abnormally small vagina can cause the same symptoms and can be corrected with surgery. The report came back showing that neither problem existed.

Then Evelyn and her husband completed a series of exercises designed to desensitize the vaginal opening so that the muscle spasm was eliminated. It's a common procedure known by qualified sex therapists. The exercises were carried out daily (a very important part of the assignment), and within three weeks they were gingerly having intercourse. She was completely cured within six weeks and experienced a climax for the first time in her life.

Once he experienced sexual satisfaction Evelyn couldn't understand why Doug didn't want to make love at every opportunity, at least twice a day! Doug had to explain to her that he couldn't do it twice a day, and she'd have to settle for three to four times a week. By their last appointment they had made a good sexual adjustment to each other.

This case was a good example of how policies of marriage can be broken out of ignorance.

The policy of honesty was violated when Evelyn failed to explain to Doug what her mother told her about sex. I was the first person who'd ever learned about her mother's sexual theories. If Doug had known what her mother encouraged her to believe, they might have done something about the problem sooner.

Protection was violated when Doug tried to make love to her knowing that she was experiencing pain. He made her condition of vaginismus worse when he continued to engage in intercourse while she was in tears. The irritation reinforced the muscle reflex, finally making penetration impossible, which is the reason he finally stopped having intercourse with her.

The exercise Doug and Evelyn used to overcome vaginismus allows just enough stimulation to be felt but not enough to create pain. If he had protected her by avoiding any pain, engaging in foreplay very gently, they probably would have solved the problem on their own. Remember, never experience pleasure at the expense of your spouse.

The policy of care was violated by both Doug and Evelyn. They both came into marriage unskilled in providing each other sexual fulfillment but made no effort to gain that skill. While this failure was largely through ignorance, Evelyn knew that she needed some guidance in understanding the problem, but she was too ashamed to discuss it with anyone. It took the threat of divorce to motivate her to do something that she should have done simply out of care.

The Procrastinator

Throughout their long marriage, Grace and Ben had been known for the affection and consideration they showed each other. No one imagined the seriousness of their marital problem. Not even Grace.

From their first anniversary on, Ben had expressed his deepest love for his beautiful and charming wife. But on their fiftieth wedding anniversary, an occasion for special appreciation for a happy and fulfilling marriage, he gave her a card that said, "Thanks for ruining my life!"

Grace thought she was having a nightmare. It was totally unexpected, and she cried for days. Ben was ashamed and begged her forgiveness. But the cat was out of the bag.

When she had finally gained enough composure to discuss the matter with him, Grace wanted him to explain himself. "Ben, this is the tenth time I've asked you this and I expect an answer. What did I do that ruined your life?"

"Please believe me," he pleaded. "I don't know what got into me. You haven't done anything. It's all my fault."

"What's all your fault?"

"Oh, it's nothing. Please forgive me for wrecking our anniversary," he insisted. "I'm just an old fool."

"*What is this all about?* I will not let you sleep until you tell me, so you may as well tell me now and get it over with."

"Okay," he agreed, "but remember, it's not your fault! All our married life, I've wanted to share sexual feelings with you. I know you've never experienced a climax with me, and sometimes I feel that I've missed out on something that's very important to me. That's all."

"Ben, I don't know how."

"Don't worry about it," he shrugged, "We're too old to do anything about it now anyway."

Throughout their marriage, Grace had not put much effort into sex. At first she didn't think it was all that important. But when it was apparent that Ben enjoyed it so much, she went through the motions just to make him happy. She always thought that some day she'd learn what it was all about. But she kept putting it off. Besides, it never occurred to her that *her* experience was an essential part of sex and that Ben couldn't be sexually fulfilled unless she experienced arousal and climax with him.

But Grace took a very important step that day. She decided to get help and made her first appointment with me that week.

I suggested she bring her husband with her next time and had them read the book, *Women's Orgasm: A Guide to Sexual Satisfaction* (New York: Graber & Graber, Warner Books, 1975). The book not only showed her how to climax, but also how to climax during intercourse, a difficult achievement for many women. They worked together on the exercises daily and hadn't ever had so much fun with each other.

Grace learned how to climax and, in a way, she was happy she'd received such a rude fiftieth anniversary card. Without it, they probably never would have shared the sexual feelings that give married couples so much pleasure and satisfaction.

Her only regret was that she'd waited so long to figure it out. The truth is, she had violated my rule of care. She failed to adequately prepare herself for one of the most important skills a spouse can possess, the ability to sexually fulfill her partner.

But Ben had made a mistake, too, by violating the policy of honesty. Through most of their marriage he was steaming. But he kept it to himself until their fiftieth wedding anniversary! He should have expressed his feelings years earlier and in a more tactful way. But sometimes honesty in any form is better than no honesty at all!

If you are a woman who isn't sure you've ever experienced a climax, or if you climax very seldom, get a copy of the book I mentioned above. If you go through the recommended exercises and still can't quite get it, consider an experienced sex therapist.

An effective sex therapist won't mind if your husband is part of each counseling session. It should be up to you. All exercises should be in the privacy of your own home either by yourself or with your husband. A therapist should never touch you or have you experience any form of sexual arousal in the office. Therapy for most sex-related marital problems is completed within three months, the cost is moderate, and the success rate is very high. We're all wired right; it's just a matter of learning where the controls are!

If you're at all uncomfortable with one therapist, go to another. Your gynecologist should be able to recommend several qualified sex therapists to you, and you may wish to consult with two or three before you settle on one.

The Narcissist

Whenever a client tells me that her husband is impotent, I'm always a little suspicious. While I've treated many men who were truly impotent, more often than not the problem turns out not to be impotence at all, but rather, excessive masturbation. I once counseled a man who brought himself to ten climaxes each day. By the time his wife wanted to make love, he was sexually exhausted! When he stopped masturbating, he had absolutely no problem at all making love to her.

But that wasn't Jerry's problem. He could do both. If Jane, his wife, ever wanted to make love, he was ready and able. He initiated lovemaking on a regular basis himself. But every once in a while she would discover evidence that he'd been masturbating. It made her furious—so much so that she made an appointment for marriage counseling.

When Jerry discussed the problem with me, he couldn't understand what her problem was. "Why should she care if I masturbate? We make love whenever she wants, don't we? And I'm an excellent lover besides. What's her problem?"

I explained to him that her feelings were what counted, and if she didn't want him to masturbate, then he shouldn't. And he also shouldn't try to hide the fact that he was doing it.

Then came the real dilemma. Jerry wasn't sure if he could

stop. Masturbation had become such a pleasurable experience for him that sex with his wife was sometimes boring in contrast. He made love to her out of duty and did a good job of it. But he looked forward to masturbating more than anything else. He felt that since no other woman was involved it was okay for him to develop a sexual procedure that brought him so much pleasure.

But Jerry actually *had* another lover: himself! And some of the same results of an affair were developing in his marriage: He was robbing his wife of the very best feelings he could have toward her. All those love units that could have been deposited in her account were squandered. I also mentioned that many men I've counseled who have serious sexual perversions—such as making obscene telephone calls and exposing in public—started with an effective program of masturbation. Perversions are usually avoided when a man brings his wife into his sexual experience.

I recommended to Jerry that, if at all possible, sexual feelings be reserved for marital lovemaking. He should avoid sexual fantasies if they didn't involve his wife, he should avoid sexual arousal if his wife were not present, and he should most certainly never experience a climax unless it was while making love to his wife. I warned her that she could expect an increase in sexual activity, and that she should try to accommodate it.

In this case, my recommendations were followed, and he was able to overcome his habit of masturbating.

The policies Jerry violated were honesty and protection. He didn't explain his sexual behavior to his wife because he knew she would object to it. The failure to be honest often hides a failure to protect. He knew his behavior would offend her, but he did it anyway because he enjoyed it. In other words, he gained at her expense. He failed to protect her and, to avoid her reaction, he didn't tell her about it.

Jerry's honesty led to a change in his behavior that protected Jane's feelings: He stopped masturbating. It also may have prevented him from forming an embarrassing and potentially career-threatening sexual perversion. But most important, it stopped the flow of love units out of his account in her Love Bank and built love units in her account. Today they're happily married!

*   *   *

We've seen in this chapter how sexual behavior can come between a husband and wife. Sex, a tool to help bring a man and woman together in marriage, can actually drive them apart when it achieves a status higher than the marriage itself or is overlooked and ignored.

When my policy of honesty is kept, a husband and wife come to understand the important differences between them, the differences in the way they are sexually aroused and come to a climax.

When my policy of protection is kept, they learn how to avoid hurting each other and try to find mutual pleasure instead. Sex is never one-sided, or at the expense of one's spouse.

When my policy of care is kept, a husband and wife learn habits and techniques that bring sexual pleasure to their spouse as well as themselves.

When my policy of time is kept, they reserve enough time to be alone so that they don't feel rushed when they make love, and they feel sexually fulfilled.

That's the way every marriage could be!

I've come to the end of the chapters that describe marital problems that are relatively easy to solve. The next three chapters of this book describe more difficult problems. They are more difficult because people have much less control over their behavior in these situations. Some destructive habits are buried so deeply that modern methods of therapy have not been very effective in dealing with them. But it's important to include these problems, because it will give you a better understanding of how the violation of my four policies is certain to destroy marriages.

But how do my policies *help* in these situations? I admit that there are not as many examples of success in solving these problems. But there are *some* successful cases, and I've chosen these to demonstrate that when my four policies are followed, even the most serious marital problems can be solved.

Twelve

How to Keep
Drug and Alcohol Addiction
From Destroying Your Marriage

Addiction is the compulsive use of a habit-forming substance. When the addict tries to stop using it, he goes through withdrawal symptoms, which can range from discomfort to death.

The word *addict* is usually applied to individuals who have developed the habit of using substances that are physically or emotionally harmful and cause particularly dangerous withdrawal symptoms. The harmful substance is used because, for a moment in time, it makes the addict feel particularly good. At first, he is willing to risk long-term health for the pleasure of the moment. But after addiction, he also uses the substance to avoid the unpleasant and dangerous withdrawal symptoms.

In marriage, addiction creates far-reaching complications. Besides being harmful to the person using the substance, it is also harmful to the spouse. The harm to the spouse can take many forms, and in this chapter I'll describe some of them. But when a married person is addicted to drugs or alcohol, it's more than a health problem: It's also a marital problem of major proportions because, one way or another, the spouse is seriously hurt.

Children are also hurt. Children of alcoholics, particularly girls, suffer greatly from the emotional turmoil of their childhood. Mental health clinics throughout America have noticed that a very high percentage of adult clients have alcoholic parents. An Iowa survey once found that about 70 percent of the daughters of alcoholic fathers had been sexually molested by their father while he'd been intoxicated.

For these and many other reasons drug and alcohol addiction destroys marriages.

Conflicts Caused by Drug and Alcohol Addiction

All four of my policies for successful marriage are broken by those who are addicted to drugs or alcohol. These violations are so predictable and so destructive that I've never seen a case in which an addict has been able to create a successful marriage for any great length of time.

Unfortunately, I have witnessed many cases in which the addiction was never controlled and the marriage either failed or suffered greatly. But the three I've chosen were successful.

1. *Using as a life-style.* Addicts are drawn to each other for the same reasons as most people: common interests. In their case the interest is drugs and alcohol. But when they break the habit some find they don't have much in common anymore—at first anyway. Norm and Ruth found that rebuilding a marriage without drugs was hard work, but it sure beat destroying it with drug addiction.
2. *Can't help lovin' that man.* Daughters of alcoholic fathers tend to be attracted to alcoholic men, even though they may be deathly afraid of them when they're intoxicated. In fact, some find that the only men they ever seem to be in love with are alcoholics. Why is this such a common problem? Can something be done to save these women from their poor judgment? Laura's experiences give us a few ideas on the subject.
3. *Drinking from the closet.* Alcoholics are usually good at

hiding their habit, but Herb was outstanding. Char knew something was wrong with their marriage, but never guessed it was gin. Fate gave her a little help one day and paved the way to a solution of their marital problems.

I've never known an addict who can follow my four policies. This is why marriages fail when one or both spouses are addicted.

One characteristic of the addict is *dishonesty*. He is dishonest with himself as well as others. As a result, it seems impossible for him to follow my first policy, honesty.

The policy of protection is violated because the addict's highest priority in life is using the addicting substance. When his use of drugs or alcohol causes pain for his spouse, he has no choice but to continue his use and let his spouse suffer.

Care is violated because he's unable to meet many of his spouse's most important marital needs while he's addicted. And time is violated because the addict is too consumed in pursuit of his drugs or alcohol to have quality time left over for his spouse.

The couples I've chosen as examples for this chapter were able to overcome their addiction and then rebuild their marriages. But even after sobriety, marriage problems are usually serious for those formerly addicted. These are the special problems that I address in the following cases:

The Matched Pair

Norm and Ruth had grown up together in the same neighborhood and fell in love while still in their early teens. He introduced her to alcohol and cigarettes and she introduced him to marijuana while they were still in grammar school. Then in junior high, whenever one came across a new drug, they would share it with the other.

They were raised by alcoholic parents and were taught at an early age about drugs and alcohol. Their home lives were wretched, but they didn't understand how their parents' addiction made it all possible.

In the eleventh grade Norm and Ruth dropped out of school and found low-paying jobs. They made enough money to support their drug habits. Selling drugs on the side and living with their parents also helped.

But after a year of relative irresponsibility, Norm was kicked out of his home and told to support himself. He invited Ruth to move into an apartment with him to help cover expenses, and for a while life was rosy. That is, until Ruth became pregnant.

Since they loved each other, they were married, and Ruth gave birth to Linda. Those two events wrecked everything. Drugs had always been their primary interest, and they had learned to respect each other's idol. But marriage and Linda interfered with all of that.

Trouble started with arguments over who was going to take care of Linda. Neither had learned too much about responsibility, and parenthood had come too fast. Norm's first solution to the problem was to stay away from home. But Ruth chased him all over town until she found him, so that strategy didn't work.

Then the arguments erupted into fights. Ruth was the first to start swinging, but she was also the first to be thrown across the room. She explained to the doctor that she had fallen on the ice. Norm was sorry that he'd lost his temper but warned her not to mess with him again.

She did "mess with him" again, and this time she went to the hospital. There was no way to conceal the abuse she'd suffered and so she did the right thing: She filed a criminal complaint for assault. Norm was arrested and convicted but given a suspended sentence on the condition that he receive therapy. It was during therapy that his addiction became apparent. His counselor convinced him that he needed treatment.

While in treatment, Norm became sober for the first time since grade school. He woke up to the world around him and saw his life for what it really was. He made an astonishing recovery. Once out of treatment, he never used drugs again, as far as I know, and he still attends Alcoholics Anonymous.

Ruth, however, was still addicted. While at first she was encouraged by his recovery, it wasn't long before he wanted her to go into treatment. It wasn't what she had in mind. Norm was becoming a real bore. He was learning how to be more responsible, but she was looking less responsible in contrast. Her favorite drinking buddy was sober. Now she had to get drunk alone, and that wasn't nearly so much fun.

One night she left him with Linda, went to a bar, and met someone whom she could drink with. By the end of the evening, she'd had sex with four different men. It was the first time she'd ever cheated on Norm. The next morning she was on the verge of suicide.

Her escapade at the bar was enough of a crisis to send Ruth to treatment. The program was as successful for her as it had been for Norm, and they were ready to begin their lives together—sober.

I saw them for the first time three years after her sobriety began. Their marriage was in shambles. They had discovered that apart from drugs and alcohol they had nothing in common. Now that they had achieved sobriety the only thing keeping them together was their love for Linda.

Having been involved in the treatment of chemical dependency for a number of years, I've known how fragile marriages are after treatment. Without a deliberate effort on the part of a treatment program, marriages often end in divorce once sobriety is achieved. In fact, some programs even encourage divorce, falsely assuming that the marriage somehow is the root of addiction.

The first point I made to Norm and Ruth was that marital compatibility is *created*. Because of their addiction, drugs had retarded their ability and motivation to create compatibility in their marriage. During their years of courting and early years of marriage, conflicts were never resolved—they were simply medicated with drugs and alcohol. They never bothered to learn to meet each other's marital needs because drugs seemed to be all they needed.

I explained to them that when they awoke from their drug-induced stupor, they discovered something that should have been no surprise: They had absolutely no marital skills. Without those skills the love units, which had been artificially created by drugs, quickly disappeared, and they didn't know how to replace them.

My second point was that they had come to the right place. I was trained in teaching couples how to *create* compatibility in their marriage. Since they didn't love each other, they would have to commit themselves to my program for three months, without any assurance that the love would ever return. At that time, they could decide if they wanted to continue marriage counseling for another three months. I wasn't certain how long it would take them to build a strong marriage, and I explained to them that it might be years.

We began with a commitment to time. I explained that they needed to set aside twenty hours each week to work on their assignments. With this time, they would give each other undivided attention, without outside interruption.

Then we worked on honesty. Treatment had taught them the importance of honesty, but they had held on to some bad habits. They were afraid that if they let each other know their true feelings, the marriage would be ruined for sure. But it wasn't. Instead, it gave them a clear understanding of each other's feelings and prepared them for the next step: learning to protect.

This goal, protection, is also difficult for those who have a history of addiction. Addicts learn self-centeredness. Learning to accommodate the feelings of others and to *give up* something just because someone else is offended by it is extremely difficult for former addicts. The flip-side, not allowing others to force you into their way of doing things, is also difficult but essential to achieve if honesty and protection are to work well together.

I was able to teach Norm and Ruth that unless they *both* felt good about any one of their habits, they were to try to eliminate it. Neither of them could use the other or allow themselves to be used. It was an exercise in assertiveness.

Finally we were ready to build compatibility by following the policy of care. We covered the marital needs that most men and women crave, and they tried to become experts at meeting the five needs most important to each of them. As expected, Norm's five needs were completely different than Ruth's.

The program of therapy worked and they loved each other by the time it was over. I warned them that over the years they would need to make revisions in their care for each other because we all change throughout life. But as long as they remained sober and kept my four policies, their marriage had a bright future.

Marrying Father

How would you like to fall in love with a type of person who leaves you for other women, is chronically unemployed, beats you, and molests your children? If your father had those characteristics, you would undoubtedly hate that behavior—but you would probably find that *type* of person attractive.

This personality type doesn't do all those horrible things as you're falling in love with him. But all the warning signs that would scare most women away get by you because you've come to overlook many of your father's less destructive alcoholic traits.

Adult daughters of alcoholic fathers have asked me from time to time to help them identify men who'd make good husbands for them. They actually bring in their boyfriends, one at a time for my opinion. I've come to realize over the years that they don't seem to find the "right" men attractive. These men don't even come close! And the type of man that I encourage them to look for is a joke to them.

Laura had been divorced five times before she made her first appointment with me, and she was only thirty-five! None of the men in her life knew that. She'd tell them that she'd been divorced only three times, and that she was twenty-eight.

The longest any marriage lasted was three years, the shortest was three months—the time it took to get the divorce. Fortunately she had no children.

Laura was in love again, and this time she wanted her marriage to work. Her fiance, Matt, had met her for the first time two months earlier. He'd also been divorced several times. He had five children from an assortment of wives and lovers but didn't have custody.

He was living with Laura because he was "temporarily" out of work and had also borrowed about a thousand dollars from her. At forty-six he was broke and a recovering alcoholic.

When I asked Laura and Matt why they thought this marriage would work when the others had failed, they explained that this time they hoped a counselor would correct the mistakes they'd made in the past.

I told Laura that the only way I could help them correct mistakes of the past was if they'd commit themselves to a supervised courtship of at least one year. They could not live together during that time, and Matt had to repay the money he borrowed.

Matt was furious.

We all make a living somehow. Some work for their pay and others don't. Matt was one of those who didn't work. He made his money living with unsuspecting women. But this woman was different than some of the others: He was in love with Laura, at least at the moment.

I told them to make another appointment when they were living in separate apartments. I didn't really expect to see them again, but three months later, there they were. Matt had found a job and moved into a rooming house. He had even paid back one hundred dollars of the money he owed Laura.

Apparently my blunt observations regarding Matt had gotten through to Laura, and she'd kicked him out. But they had enough love for each other to try my plan of courtship.

I began their counseling by pointing out the obvious: The

reason their marriages had failed in the past was that they were more concerned with what they'd *get* than with what they had to *give*. Their marital *needs* motivated them to marry, but their inability to *meet* marital needs guaranteed divorce.

They both seemed willing to learn, and my four policies for successful marriage guided the adventure.

Honesty was the first hurdle. Laura finally admitted that she was divorced five times, not three, and that she was thirty-five, not twenty-eight.

Matt admitted that he had served time in prison for assaulting one of his former wives, that he had originally been interested in Laura so that she'd support him financially. He also revealed that one of his children would not see him because he had beaten him so badly two years earlier.

He was willing to answer any and all questions that she had for him and allowed her to speak to any of his former wives, girlfriends, children, relatives, or friends. I encouraged her to take him up on his offer and gather as much information as she could from the people who knew him at various times in his life.

I explained to Matt and Laura that all his irresponsible behavior, much of it done while he was using drugs, reflected a basic self-centeredness that he had not yet overcome. The fact that he'd been sober for two years was only the first step toward preparing for marriage. He had many steps to go.

Matt was encouraged to do a background check on Laura too. Each man he spoke to told him that she was great to be with until they were married; then she turned into a witch. Even her brother and sisters told him that she was incredibly hard to get along with.

I kept reminding them that the best prediction of the future is found in the past. Unless tremendous effort is made, we all tend to make the same mistakes throughout life.

With honesty accomplished, we then took a look at the habits that would provide protection. Both Matt and Laura had a long history of violent behavior. They were also in the habit of getting their way at the expense of others and making demands. All these habits had to change.

While working on protection, we started considering the skills they would need to build to provide care for each other. The most obvious skill he needed was learning to provide consistent financial support. He also needed to learn to share all financial decisions with her. Having been accustomed to putting money he earned into his own pocket, he had to learn to put his paycheck into a joint checking account that required both of their signatures.

Laura needed to learn to be less critical and to provide admiration. The men in her life had so many serious problems that she didn't believe men *could* be admired. Even though she loved Matt, it took her quite a while to learn to compliment him. They worked on other skills as well and within a year had done a good job preparing for their marriage.

There were many moments when they were ready to give up. He was particularly upset over the prospect of supporting her financially for the rest of his life when she had a job that paid more than his. But she explained to him that she wanted him to be able to pay for all of their living expenses, and she wanted her salary to go for vacations, emergencies, and saving for a home.

I've always maintained that agreements made *before* marriage are much easier to keep than those made *after* marriage. Since Matt's employment was a *condition* to their marriage, he kept it. Laura learned to meet his needs as well, by preagreement. None of her former husbands would have believed the changes she made. Demands were out—admiration was in.

So far, the marriage has worked for Matt and Laura. She married a man who was very much like her father, but he was able to overcome some of her father's more destructive habits. I think his age had a lot to do with their success. If he had been much younger, I'm not sure he would have been willing to go through the ordeal.

The Closet Alcoholic

While most psychologists are trained to identify people at risk for alcoholism, the layman isn't. As a result, very few people know whether or not their spouses are likely to be addicted to drugs or alcohol.

Herb was at risk, but his wife, Char, didn't know it. They had both been raised in a religious setting where the use of alcohol was strictly forbidden. The idea that Herb could become an alcoholic seemed preposterous.

It all started in high school. At a party one evening, Herb had his first taste of alcohol. He drank too much but was able to get home and in bed without his parents knowing that he'd been drunk. The same thing happened on a few other occasions, and while his closest school friends knew what was going on, none of them went to his church.

When Herb married Char, she never knew about his drinking in high school. Since he knew she was against all alcoholic beverages, he never dared drink in her presence.

As an attorney, it wasn't too difficult for Herb to figure out ways to slip gin, his favorite drink, into his office. There, he would drink enough to satisfy his addiction but not enough to be drunk or to cause failure in the performance of his duties.

Over a period of years their marriage suffered. Herb spent very little time at home, and when he was there he had a very low tolerance for conflict. Char wasn't able to understand what was bothering him. She knew he was under constant pressure at work and thought that his emotional distance was caused by being preoccupied with his work. Since she had never tasted alcohol herself or known anyone who drank, she never knew when he'd been drinking. He was quiet at home most of the time anyway, and his silence was a great way to avoid discovery when he had too much to drink.

At first, Herb did all his drinking at work, but after a few years, he discovered a way to drink at home. He took a bottle of windshield washer fluid, emptied it, and put in a gallon of gin with blue food coloring. He kept the bottle in the closet near his garage. It worked like a charm. Each time he felt like having a drink, he stepped into the closet and took a swig.

Both at work and at home Herb was falling farther and farther into the pit of addiction. Char found him increasingly hostile, distant, and unempathetic. He seemed to have lost his personality somewhere along the line. She spent many days in tears, reflecting on the nightmare her marriage had become. Yet she couldn't understand why it was turning out so badly.

One day it all became clear. Herb's brother, Rob, came over to the house during the morning to borrow a baseball and bat. While he was there, he put what he thought was windshield washer fluid into his car. When he returned the ball and bat that afternoon, he also returned with a new gallon of windshield washer fluid to replace what he had taken. Herb came home that night and took a swig of the real thing. He swallowed it before he realized it wasn't gin.

Herb went into a blind panic. He thought he was about to die! Char came running to find him more talkative than he'd been in years.

"I drank this windshield washer! Quick get me to the hospital!" he shouted.

She was bewildered. "Why'd you do that? Were you trying to kill yourself?"

"No. I thought it was gin. Quick, get me to the hospital."

"You thought it was gin? I don't understand. . . ."

"*Never mind!* Just get me to the hospital, quick!"

At the hospital Herb's stomach was pumped, and he was sent home. But he believed that God had put him through that ordeal to teach him a lesson. He knew he was an alcoholic and so he admitted himself to a treatment program the next day. Char was completely overwhelmed.

While he was in treatment, Char asked me to help her sort it all out. I explained to her how this sort of thing happens and, more importantly, how it affected their marriage. Herb's unwillingness to face conflict, his emotional distance, his lack of empathy, and his apparent disinterest in her and the family were all symptoms of alcoholism. Some people have those characteristics when they're sober, but for Herb they were out of character.

Withdrawal was very difficult for him, and following treatment he was very tempted to sneak gin again. Then he joined Alcoholics Anonymous. At the same time he joined Char for marriage counseling.

She was able to explain to him what had been missing in their marriage. I suggested that his addiction had made it impossible for him to meet her marital needs. They spent several weeks catching up on a lifetime of misinformation.

Herb went back to his high school days and explained how he'd fooled everyone, including Char. He went on to tell her about his deepest feelings—how important she and their family really were to him now that alcohol was not coming between them.

Herb's violation of the honesty policy was the most significant cause of their marital disruption. It set up violations of all the other policies. When honesty finally entered their relationship, protection, care, and time quickly followed.

Through honesty, Herb overcame his addiction, eliminating the most important barrier to his protection of Char. Now he could honestly tell her how he felt and what he was doing, knowing that it met with her approval and was not at her expense.

And his willingness to tell her what he felt met one of her most important marital needs—conversation. It created emotional intimacy that Char had been lacking for years, and through it Herb was showing care for her.

*   *   *

There are many suffering marriages in which one spouse *knows* that addiction is the culprit but can't convince the addicted spouse to commit to treatment. A procedure known as an "intervention" is often the only way to wake up the offending spouse. Friends, relatives, the employer, children, and the nonaddicted spouse are brought together with the help of a chemical dependency specialist to confront the addicted spouse with the problems that are being created by the addiction. Immediate treatment is recommended, and I've witnessed many cases where, after the intervention, the addicted spouse is willingly admitted to a treatment program.

The danger in such a procedure is that even after successful treatment, the addicted spouse can harbor permanent resentment toward those who put him through the intervention. I've known of cases (not conducted in any of my clinics) where, after intervention has failed, the addicted spouse committed suicide, blaming everyone who tried to intervene for his or her death.

I've found that one of the safest and most effective ways to get the addicted spouse into treatment is for him to be arrested for Driving While Intoxicated (DWI) and have a judge sentence him to treatment. Many judges recognize the unique position they're in to help solve one of the greatest problems of society and marriage. I look to the judicial system for increasing help in solving one of marriage's greatest problems, drug and alcohol addiction.

Clearly, drug and alcohol addiction comes between a husband and wife. The addiction itself is a higher priority than marriage and, as a result, my four policies are impossible to keep. But even after sobriety is achieved, many of the bad habits acquired during addiction persist, and the policies are continually violated.

In most marriages where at least one spouse has been addicted, learning to keep my four policies is an essential requirement for marital success. But in many cases, even after sobriety, many *choose* not to follow the rules. For example, an incredibly high percentage of people have affairs with those they met while in treatment. Sobriety is no guarantee of marital success, but addiction guarantees marital failure.

In this chapter I selected cases where marriages were saved because the couple *chose* to put each other first and follow my four policies. But I don't want you to be under any illusions: The marriages of most addicts fail, even after sobriety is achieved.

It takes commitment to my policies and hard work to turn these marriages around. But you are at a distinct advantage: Now, at least, you know the rules!

Thirteen

How to Keep
Infidelity
From Destroying Your Marriage

Among the most cruel, destructive, and perverse marital practices, infidelity probably tops the list. Only child molestation comes close to the rage and disgust experienced by the offended spouse. And yet, we find infidelity to be rampant in our society— even recommended by some so-called experts in counseling.

The emotional pain suffered by the offended spouse is often worse than being beaten and worse than rape. How can so many people inflict that kind of pain on the ones they promised to cherish?

Infidelity usually begins with the vacuum created by an unmet marital need. In other words, a violation of my policy, care, can create the climate for an affair. The unmet marital needs that drive most men to an affair are: sexual fulfillment, recreational companionship, an attractive spouse, domestic support, and admiration. For most women they are: affection, conversation, honesty and openness, financial support, and family commitment. (See chapter 5 for a fuller explanation of these needs.) When *any* of these marital needs are *unmet*, people may be tempted to have an affair.

But failure to care by one spouse is no excuse for the other spouse's failure to protect. If a man's sexual needs are not being met by his wife, he has no right or excuse to have sex with someone else. He should solve his problem without breaking any of my four policies. And infidelity clearly breaks the policy of protection. It's a solution for him that's at her expense.

Men are twice as likely to have an affair as women, and they seem to be less willing to end the affair when there's hope for saving their marriage. When a man sees me for marriage counseling, usually to placate his wife, I first counsel him apart from his wife, encouraging him to end the affair. But I generally don't begin marriage counseling until I'm convinced the affair is over.

Infidelity is like an addiction. It's a compulsive, mindless dependence. The highest priority of an unfaithful spouse is being with his lover. He thinks about her constantly and needs to call her to be reassured that she's still available to him. His need to be with her is a higher priority than the feelings of his wife. Even when he knows that his affair can cause his wife pain, he continues at her expense. As a result, he cannot keep my policy of protection.

He cannot keep my policy of honesty, either. Infidelity leads people to be incredibly dishonest. Until the addiction is over-come, they experience lapses of dishonesty to preserve the addiction. Since they are unable to keep the policies of honesty and protection, there is no hope to restore the marriage until the affair has ended.

While honesty is the first step toward the solution of all marital problems, when the problem is infidelity, honesty is incredibly difficult to obtain. Somehow, people have the idea that once an affair is known, all hope of reconciliation is gone.

Some counselors, who understand the pain that infidelity creates, help sustain the deception by suggesting that affairs, past or present, be left undisclosed. In other words, they suggest that you should break my policy of honesty if it's likely to cause too much pain.

I don't agree with these counselors. I've seen repeatedly that truth is the first step in avoiding *future* pain. Truth helps you understand the circumstances that create the pain, enabling you to avoid it in the future. If you're having an affair, or if you've ever had an affair, don't keep it from your spouse. Explain it, even if you think the problems have been resolved. Withholding truth is monumentally shortsighted!

If you ever have a conflict between my policies of honesty and protection, when truth causes pain, choose honesty. You may lose some love units at first, but truth is the first step toward solving marital problems. Without honesty you'll be unable to achieve protection and care. Honesty by itself won't solve your marital problems, but without it you can't even *begin* to solve them.

In this chapter, I won't be able to unravel the mystery of affairs as I did in my book, *His Needs, Her Needs: Building an Affair-proof Marriage.* But we'll study three cases that show how infidelity destroys marriages due to the violation of my four policies. Then I'll show you how these marriages were restored when the policies were followed.

1. *Charity begins at home.* Some people take caring for widows far too seriously! Nate was so willing to help people in his neighborhood that he could be summoned in a flash. His wife, Cheryl, was praised by her friends for having such a kind and generous husband. But when she discovered that his generosity included sex, she was no longer flattered.
2. *Wives raise children, secretaries make love.* Dean's secretary was not only a good typist, but also a good lover. In fact, almost all of his secretaries were good lovers. After two divorces he finally figured out why his marriages were so fragile—and why his secretaries were so attractive!
3. *Too much in common.* Beth and Harry shared many common interests, including an interest in men. Beth discovered that infidelity is not limited to opposite-sex partners when she found that her husband, an accoun-

tant, was having sex with one of his *male* clients. She claimed that if his lover had been a woman, it might have been easier to handle. She's probably right!

Infidelity, like drug and alcohol addiction, causes an inability to follow my four policies. I've never been able to help a using addict save his marriage and I've rarely been able to help someone in an ongoing affair, either. I'm usually successful only after the affair is ended.

The couples we'll study in this chapter were able to end their affairs, and my job was to help them rebuild their marriages and make them less vulnerable to another affair.

The Willing Worker

Cheryl wasn't getting any younger and was starting to worry if she'd ever find a man who could meet her standards. Then she discovered Nate. He was the most incredibly helpful and thoughtful person she'd ever known. He fixed her car, he fixed her washing machine, he mowed her lawn, and he painted one of her rooms. He did anything she'd tell him to do. What a man!

Within a year, they were married. Two years later they had their first child. Cheryl had no idea what a mess children could make, and she was thrilled to have married a man who'd help her make dinner and clean up the house after he came home from work. Every evening she'd make a list of things for him to do that would keep him busy until bedtime. Weekends were also filled with projects. She was delighted to see so many things accomplished within such short spaces of time. But she rarely told him how much she appreciated his work. And if he ever complained about all the work he had to do, she'd become angry.

Cheryl was violating my policy of protection by making demands and the policy of care by failing to meet his needs for domestic support or admiration. She was happier than a clam— at his expense. While he was gaining love units in her Love Bank, she was *losing* love units in his.

Over a period of time, however, Cheryl found Nate helping the neighbors with their household projects more than he was helping her. In fact, he became a legend in his neighborhood because he was such a skilled repairman and was always willing to help. The neighbors praised Nate for his helpfulness and Cheryl for her willingness to put off her own projects so that he could help others.

One day, Norma, a neighbor whose husband had died three years earlier, called Cheryl to ask a favor. "I hate to bother you, but something's wrong with my water heater. I haven't been able to find a repairman to fix it this weekend, and I was wondering if Nate would be willing to look at it for me?"

"Oh, certainly," said Cheryl. "I'll send him right over."

Within an hour, Nate had fixed Norma's water heater. But he didn't stop there. He also fixed her garbage disposal unit and her garage door opener. By the time he was ready to leave, she was in tears.

"I can't tell you how much this has meant to me. Since Roger died, I've had one problem after another, with no one to help me. And I've been so lonely. You've made me happier than I've been in years." She gave him a big hug.

Nate was speechless, but he hugged her back. Before he left he told her that if she ever needed help, all she'd have to do is give him a call.

Norma called Nate that next Saturday, and he was right over, helping her clean up a pile of leaves that had been rotting in a corner of the front yard for two years. When he was ready to go, she invited him inside for coffee, and they spent three hours talking to each other. She shared many of the struggles a widow faces, among them, her loneliness and sexual frustration. He shared with her some of his problems, which included Cheryl's constant demands and lack of appreciation. By the end of the conversation they were making love.

Slowly but surely, Cheryl's love units had been withdrawn from Nate's Love Bank. Every time she gave him work to do he was offended. Once in a while he would tell her how he felt, but when he did she'd tell him that she hated lazy men. A compliment would have meant so much to him. But she took his help for granted and failed to meet one of his most important marital needs—admiration.

Another need Cheryl failed to meet was domestic support, since Nate did most of the housework for her. Norma picked up on both of these failures and showered him with praise. She also had something cooked for him whenever he came over.

While Nate's excuse for being with Norma was helping her with a project, he actually spent very little of his time working. Instead they talked to each other and made love. When he did repair something, she was always with him, telling him how much she appreciated his effort.

Cheryl didn't suspect a thing. When Nate came home, he got right to work on his own projects and didn't go to bed until they were completed.

Over the next six months, however, Nate began to neglect his own home. Cheryl's lists of projects began to gather dust, and Nate was with Norma several times a week. Norma praised every effort he made on her behalf, and he just loved all the attention he was getting from her. They made love two or three times a week but were very careful so that they wouldn't be discovered. Love units were pouring into her account in his Love Bank.

Cheryl eventually became suspicious, particularly when their own sexual relationship started to fall apart. Nate claimed to have lost interest in sex. She finally confronted him, but he lied about his relationship with Norma.

Over the next two years Cheryl tried very hard to determine if Nate was having an affair with Norma. She never caught them making love but appeared at Norma's house unannounced on several occasions. Nate finally became alarmed with her increasingly suspicious behavior. He told her that if it would make her happy he wouldn't help Norma any longer. That apparent concession made Cheryl much more relaxed—at least until Norma's neighbor called several weeks later.

Nate and Norma were seen driving into Norma's garage, her neighbor reported. She thought Cheryl should know about it.

Cheryl walked right over and found them together. Now she *knew* Nate was having an affair and insisted that he see a marriage counselor. He agreed to go with her but continued to deny that he was having an affair.

My first conversation with Nate was typical. He simply couldn't be pinned down. He told me that his wife was perfect, he was happily married, and that he merely had compassion for a widow in the neighborhood.

I told Cheryl that I wanted to counsel Nate alone for a few weeks before I could begin marriage counseling, and they agreed to that plan. The very next time I saw Nate, he told me about his relationship with Norma but made me promise I wouldn't tell Cheryl about it. We discussed the pros and cons of marital reconciliation, and within three weeks he decided to save his marriage.

Nate's primary motive for reconciliation was his three children. He loved Norma more than Cheryl but realized he had a lot to lose in a divorce. Besides, he knew that Norma wouldn't be able to meet some of his other marital needs. She wasn't nearly as attractive as Cheryl, and they didn't have very many interests in common. He knew he couldn't marry her, even if he were divorced.

Nate's first assignment was to tell Cheryl that she'd been right about his affair, but that he'd decided to leave that relationship and rebuild his marriage. Even though she had known it all along she took it very hard.

I recommended that Nate and Cheryl move. He had invested thousands of hours into his home, and it was hard for him to even think of selling it. But I felt that the home represented a way of life that had enslaved him and that a new home would give them a fresh start. I also didn't feel he could be trusted living so close to Norma, and that was the most important reason to move.

Nate and Cheryl eventually sold their home and moved twenty miles away, far enough so that he could avoid seeing Norma but close enough to his job that he wouldn't need to find another.

We began marriage counseling with an emphasis on honesty. Nate had never shared his deepest feelings with Cheryl, and he used work to help him remain superficial. I taught him how to talk to her and recommended that, for the next few weeks, he spend all his time at home talking rather than working.

In his conversations with Cheryl, he told her how unhappy he'd been with her lack of appreciation. She explained that she had the greatest admiration for him but had simply taken him for granted and had neglected to tell him how much she appreciated him.

Cheryl's lists of projects that she'd given him were a violation of my policy of protection. She learned to ask how he felt about doing them, and Nate learned to tell her the truth about how he felt. To her surprise, she discovered that when he came home from work, he wanted her to have dinner ready and the house cleaned. He preferred watching television to completing one of her projects! But when he did agree to do something for her, she realized that it was an act of care on his part, and she learned to compliment him for it.

Nate learned to be honest with Cheryl; she learned to avoid criticism and express her appreciation. They started a new life together.

Instead of spending all his time on projects around the house, Nate used some of it to be alone with Cheryl and they gave each other undivided attention. They already had countless interests in common and had little difficulty enjoying recreational activities together. Time made it possible. Their sexual relationship had never been a problem until Norma came on the scene. Again, time helped bring back a fulfilling sexual relationship for both of them.

Cheryl was already deeply in love with Nate, but the new

program made her realize that her household projects not only kept her from meeting his needs but also had kept him from meeting two of her most important marital needs—conversation and honesty. Two years later she told me that her marriage was better than it had ever been and that her resentment toward Nate had disappeared. And Nate was in love with Cheryl again. She lost a repairman but gained a husband!

Mixing Pleasure with Business

Dean's first marriage was great until children arrived. Then he had an affair with his secretary, whom he later married. You'd think that he'd learned something from the failure of his first marriage. But, no.

When his second wife had a child, he had an affair with another secretary, divorced his second wife, and came to see me for counseling. He couldn't understand what made his marriages so fragile and his secretaries so appealing!

Upon examination the answer was clear.

His first wife, Ellen, had been a constant companion and devoted friend while they were dating. They'd grown up together and fully expected to be married for life. But he expected her to give him undivided attention, which she willingly did right up to the time she had their first child. Then her attention was turned from him to the child. Two more children made matters worse.

Dean knew he wasn't happy with her shift of interest but loved his children and wanted them to have all the attention they needed from their mother. He'd become a successful business-man and had his own private secretary, Kim. She was paid to give him attention and, in the process, became his closest friend—and eventually his lover.

Ellen never did discover his affair with Kim, but after their divorce and his eventual marriage to Kim, she suspected it. He simply told her that they'd "grown apart" and he no longer loved her. She could do nothing to stop the divorce.

Kim didn't continue as his secretary after their marriage.

Instead, she wanted to raise children, which Dean encouraged. But after their first child arrived, Dean struck up a deep friendship with his new private secretary, Joan. Needless to say, by the time their second child arrived, Dean was in love with Joan and divorced Kim—who was totally surprised! She didn't suspect Joan because Dean had always told her that she wasn't his type. But after their divorce she knew he'd lied!

Before Dean married a third time, he felt it would be helpful to consult a marriage counselor. He'd already seen the pattern, and he wanted Joan to be his third and *last* wife. What could he do to avoid a third divorce?

As with most cases of infidelity, Dean's marital needs were not being met. His wives had violated my third policy—care. They'd shifted their attention from caring for him to caring for their children. During courtship and early marriage they had met his needs, so they certainly knew how to do it. But children changed their priorities, and Dean took a back seat to children that he loved too. Since he wanted them to have the best care, instead of complaining, he simply had his needs met by someone else.

To make his plan work, he had to violate my first policy—honesty. He lied so effectively that neither of his first two wives ever suspected him of infidelity until it was too late.

He also violated my policy of protection. If he had been honest about his plans, either wife would have objected and he knew it. But he did it anyway because he was willing to meet his needs even if it was at their expense.

My policy of time was violated by Dean and his former wives. They all failed to understand the importance of their time alone; children came between them. Before marriage and before children, they spent almost every spare moment alone with each other. After children, they were hardly ever alone.

After explaining to Dean how his marriages failed, I asked him to let Joan join the counseling sessions. I wanted him to explain it to her while I listened to be sure he didn't leave anything out.

Dean told her that he'd lied to both of his former wives and had already lied to her about a few things. The policy of honesty would be very difficult for him to keep, since he had established a habit of lying to the women in his life.

The policy of protection, he thought, would be much easier for him. But because he had a history of dishonesty, it had not been tested. Whenever he wanted to do something that his wife would dislike, he simply lied about it.

He knew how to meet a woman's marital needs (care), but after children, he wouldn't give his wife enough of his time for them to be met. Dean promised Joan that if she married him, he would give her at least fifteen hours of his undivided attention every week or see a marriage counselor immediately.

Over the next few counseling sessions, Dean explained to Joan how he felt toward his wives while having affairs with his secretaries. He cared about them and never thought the affairs would lead to divorce. He even thought that they were good for his marriage, since they helped him overcome resentment.

Love was something that Dean never quite understood. He felt that he should marry women he loved and divorce women he no longer loved. He began to understand that love is created and destroyed in a relationship and that he had quite a bit of control over what direction it took.

At our last counseling session, I recommended that Dean and Joan practice my four policies to prove that they can do it. They've been married for about ten years now, and the last I heard, the marriage has been very successful. Joan had no children, and she still plays an active role in his business as his secretary and lover . . . and wife.

The Big Surprise

Until the AIDS epidemic of recent years, most people were unaware of how widespread homosexual relationships have become. Counselors see an increasing number of men and women who are guilt-ridden over their same-sex attraction and want to be "cured." I've seen priests, pastors, Boy Scout leaders, and others who are repulsed by their sexual orientation and desperately wish to overcome it.

For those with no homosexual leanings it's a bizarre phenomenon. But if surveys are even close to being accurate, about 25 percent of all men and women are sexually attracted to both sexes (bisexual), and 10 percent are strongly attracted to the same sex (homosexual). My own surveys find that about 10 percent of men and women have actually engaged in some form of homosexual activity during their late teen and early adult years. In other words, it's fairly common to be homosexual, but its effects on individuals and marriages are devastating.

Since many homosexual men and women marry the opposite sex, a characteristic problem develops in their marriages: homosexual infidelity. In many ways the causes of infidelity are the same, whether homosexual or heterosexual. But homosexual infidelity has problems of its own. For this reason, and because the condition is so widespread, I include this case.

Beth had dated only once before meeting Harry. But on their first date, she was certain that he was the one for her. They seemed to have identical interests in art, music, politics, religion—almost everything. What she didn't realize was that they were both sexually attracted to men as well!

Harry was a closet homosexual. He was ashamed of his sexual orientation and wanted to develop a good relationship with a woman so he'd look "normal." Besides, he was planning to become an accountant and believed he ought to have a family in order to be accepted by the business community.

While Harry was affectionate to Beth during courtship, he made very few sexual advances. Beth was opposed to premarital sex, so his lack of heterosexual interest was never discovered. He started the relationship violating my policy of honesty.

On their wedding night Harry had a great deal of trouble achieving arousal, and he was finally successful only after imagining Beth was a man. The fantasy worked so well that he used it each time he made love to her from that day on. But he didn't tell her about it, again violating my policy of honesty.

Harry finished college and became an accountant. Over the next few years, they had three children and their marriage was great as far as Beth was concerned. Harry knew that he was homosexual, but didn't let anyone know for fear he'd be ridiculed and lose some of his business.

Harry might have gone through life with his secret had it not been for Ray, another businessman in town and one of his clients, who was also homosexual. Harry was working with Ray on a tax problem one Saturday when the subject of homosexuality came up. Ray admitted to Harry that he was gay, and in a moment of abandon, Harry revealed that he was, too. One thing led to another and, within a month, Harry had sex with Ray. In so doing, Harry violated my policy of protection, as well as his vow of faithfulness.

Harry was in my office a month or so later, ready to end it all.

"Why did God make me this way? I've asked Him to change my sexual desires, even get rid of them altogether!"

"Apparently, God wants you to work on the problem," I suggested.

"I've tried, and look what a mess I'm in now."

"But you didn't go about it the right way. You've been incredibly dishonest. How do you expect to solve your problems that way?"

"If I tell people what happened, I'll lose everything—my business, my marriage, my children, everything." Then he broke down and cried.

I continued counseling him for a few weeks, and finally he was ready to tell his wife what had happened. I knew she'd need counseling herself and saw them both the day after he revealed his indiscretion.

She was absolutely torn apart by his revelation. After crying all night and threatening to divorce him, she finally calmed down enough to look at the problem somewhat objectively. But it took several weeks before she was able to sleep at night.

I encouraged Harry to tell her everything: his sexual fantasy when they made love, his prayers to God for deliverance, and his attachment to Ray and other men. For the first time in their relationship he was totally honest with Beth. While it was all overwhelming, he could never have developed intimacy with her until he shared his deepest feelings. Once he'd explained his feelings, they were ready to deal with their problem.

While violating the policy of honesty kept Harry and Beth from solving this marital problem, once they followed the policy, they were able to consider a solution. He became thoroughly convinced that his deception had been unfair to his wife. He should have told her about his homosexual orientation *before* they were married. So he vowed to make every effort to keep her informed of the truth for the remainder of their marriage.

They both understood that Harry had been unfaithful, that he violated his exclusive sexual agreement with Beth. But it was also a violation of the protection policy. Harry made a commitment to take Beth's feelings into account before he acted and to avoid gaining at her expense.

Part of the reason that Harry was unfaithful was that his sexual needs were not being met. We already indicated that if a spouse is dishonest, care is impossible to achieve. So Beth had no chance to meet this marital need. But even if he had been honest, how can a woman ever meet a man's sexual need when he's more attracted to men?

I gave Harry an assignment that gave Beth the opportunity to provide the care he needed. It's an assignment I recommend to all married couples: *Include your spouse in all of your sexual experiences.* Every sexual fantasy, every sexual act, every sexual climax.

As a marriage counselor, I've always been impressed by how quickly sex builds love units. Sex is one of the least expensive and most effortless ways to enjoy each other. Why waste it on someone or something else?

Harry didn't think he could do the assignment because of his habit of masturbation, with men as the objects of his fantasies. But he quickly discovered that if he didn't masturbate, but made love to his wife whenever he was sexually inclined, he could think about her and be sexually aroused. He didn't need a homosexual fantasy after all.

Within a few weeks, Harry had learned to *let* Beth meet his need for sexual fulfillment.

Even after learning to focus sexual interest in his wife, Harry was still homosexual. He still finds men more sexually attractive than women. But he's learned to invest his sexual interest and energy in his wife, and he has enough heterosexual drive to let Beth meet his sexual need.

Beth has a much better marriage now than she had before. Harry's dishonesty ruined their chances for true sexual compatibility. But by being honest and recommitting sexual exclusiveness to his wife, Harry found that he could be sexually fulfilled by her after all.

Beth was an unusually tolerant and committed wife. She wanted to save their marriage, even after learning of her husband's infidelity and homosexual orientation; she was willing to be the very best sex partner she could be; she made personal concessions to make sex enjoyable for Harry.

I've discovered, time and time again, that honesty brings the very best out of people, and dishonesty brings out the worst. While my policy of honesty doesn't solve marital problems by itself, they are impossible to solve without it!

*   *   *

Infidelity violates all four of my policies for successful marriage. Marriage cannot be restored until the unfaithfulness ends, because the rules *cannot* be followed. Any man or woman who thinks they can draw their spouse out of an affair is sadly mistaken. In any addiction, the addict is the only one who can set himself free. In the same way, the unfaithful spouse is the only one who can separate himself from his lover.

But in most marriages, even after an affair has ended, the causes of the affair persist and make future affairs likely. Marriages *can* be restored. Couples must simply choose to follow my four policies. When they do, their marriages are protected against future affairs.

I selected three cases in this chapter where couples chose to put each other first and follow my policies. I've seen many others do the same, with restored marriages. But I've also witnessed many cases where, consciously and deliberately, couples refused to follow these policies, and they've fallen back into infidelity.

The choice is up to you. These policies can save marriages that even infidelity has nearly destroyed.

Fourteen
How to Keep
Emotional Disorders
From Destroying Your Marriage

Those trained in my profession, clinical psychology, help people gain control over emotions which have overcome them. These emotions usually make them unhappy and unable to function properly. When they've lost emotional control, emotions instead of intelligence guide their thoughts, plans, and behavior. When that happens, their lives are in shambles.

When someone comes to me for help, they're usually suffering from one of three emotional disorders: depression, anxiety, or anger. Of course, there are many who suffer from two, or even all three.

Depression is the feeling of hopelessness: nothing to look forward to; no reason to go on; things will never get better, only worse; my best years are behind me, my worst years are ahead.

When depression controls you, you're convinced that planning is pointless because no plan will ever work for you anyway. And even if you have a plan, trying hard to achieve it is foolish because you'll fail regardless of your efforts. In other words, depression *makes* you fail because it overrides the intelligence that *knows how* you can succeed.

Anxiety is the fear of impending doom: fear of flying because the plane may crash; fear of elevators because they may fall; fear of enclosed spaces because escape may be impossible; fear of the unknown because you never know what's finally going to get you.

When anxiety controls you, you're convinced that disaster is right around the corner. It may not be *this* corner, but some day, it will get you right between the eyes. The emotion tends to convince people that they shouldn't go around *any* corner of life, just to be safe. In other words, anxiety immobilizes you, because it overrides the intelligence that knows that the problem that lurks around the corner can be solved and won't defeat you.

Anger is the feeling that your unhappiness is caused by people who will keep upsetting you until they're punished: They can't be reasoned with; the only thing they understand is pain and personal loss. Once you inflict that punishment, they'll think twice about making you unhappy again!

When anger controls you, you're convinced that someone or something is *making* you feel miserable. If you can get him to stop, you'll feel much better. Furthermore, if you can punish him enough, which he deserves, he'll never try to make you feel miserable again.

Anger convinces people that the solution to their troubles is to punish the troublemaker. Anger overrides the intelligence that knows that punishment doesn't solve problems; it only makes the people you punish angry and causes them to inflict punishment on you! And when you become angry with your spouse, it overrides the intelligence that wants you to show care and protection. Anger wants you to hurt the one you love the most.

All three of these emotions are normal. We all feel depressed, anxious, and angry once in a while. But when they begin to take over our lives, then the emotions become *emotional disorders*, conditions that psychologists and other mental health specialists are trained to help people overcome.

Emotional disorders are not only unpleasant for those who have them. They're also unpleasant for the spouses of those who have them. Can you imagine what it would be like living with someone who is depressed, or anxious, or angry most of the time?

In many of the cases of marital conflict that I see, the most important cause of incompatibility is the uncontrolled emotions of one or both spouses. These emotions come between them. Their emotions, rather than their intelligence, guide their behavior. Then they become unable to solve the simplest marital conflicts.

Before I begin marriage counseling, I give every couple an emotional assessment to see if the emotions of either spouse are out of control. If they are, I usually treat them individually until that control is achieved, and then I begin marriage counseling. When I work with a couple's intelligence, my job is very rewarding. But when all I have is emotions, marriage counseling wastes my time and theirs.

Conflicts Caused by Emotional Disorders

There are innumerable causes for emotional disorders. Sometimes they're inherited; sometimes they're caused by a rotten childhood; sometimes they're caused by a frustrating job, or financial pressures, or an unfulfilling marriage. Whatever the reasons, their effect on marriage is almost always negative.

Those who experience emotional disorders usually violate my first policy—honesty. They don't want people to know about their history of emotional struggle, for fear they won't be accepted. They often keep their feelings to themselves because they don't want to be a burden on others or they don't want people to think they're weird. The things they do to try to keep their emotions under control are often hidden from the world, and they tend to be lonely and isolated, even when married.

People with emotional disorders also violate the policy of protection. Someone who is constantly angry, for example, consciously and deliberately punishes those who make them feel bad, particularly the spouse. Cases of battering, in which a man beats his wife, are almost always caused by anger disorders.

Those who are depressed or who suffer from anxiety engage in countless annoying habits in an effort to reduce their emotional symptoms. For example, depression often keeps people from going to work, maintaining physical hygiene, or picking up after themselves. One depressed man I counseled, complaining about his wife's lack of sexual interest, had not bathed for three months!

My policy against making demands is almost always violated by those with emotional disorders. Since emotions are guiding their planning, their requests don't make any sense, and when their requests fail, demands quickly take over. They often feel so bad and their intelligence is so overcome by emotions that demands are the only way they can communicate.

My policy of care is violated by those with emotional disorders, because their own unhappiness makes caring extremely difficult for them. They are so consumed in their own emotions that they have little to invest in the needs of others, including their spouses.

Finally, my policy of time is violated for the same reason that care is violated: Emotional disorders make people self-centered, and they have great difficulty giving someone else their undivided attention. When they spend time alone with their spouse, their attention is focused inward and they appear preoccupied.

But emotional disorders can be overcome. The first step is the recognition that an emotion is leading you astray and that you want your intelligence to be in control once again. When you take that step, there are many methods available to psychologists that are effective in overcoming emotional bondage, and it's simply a matter of getting help from a qualified psychologist or other mental health specialist.

I've witnessed hundreds of people with emotional disorders who've gained lifelong control over their emotions and restored their marriages. The following cases will give you a sample involving depression, anxiety, and anger.

1. *Marrying one for the price of two.* Howard was the life of the party when Joy first met him. But after they married

he became the death of the party. Joy thought she was to blame until she discovered his long history of bouts with depression. Howard had the choice of doing something about them or losing Joy.

2. *There's no place like home.* It's one thing to like housework, but quite another to never leave the house! Valerie had so many fears that the safest thing to do was to stay at home, which she did for three years. In some cultures, men would have considered her the perfect wife. But not in ours! When her husband finally had all he could take, she got up the courage to overcome her fear. It opened up a new life for her and saved her marriage.

3. *No way to treat a lady.* Carolyn liked Norm because he was decisive. He knew what he wanted and he got what he wanted. He wanted Carolyn, so they were married. But she had a rude awakening when she discovered what he did when he *didn't* get what he wanted: He flew into a rage! She had the sense to leave him after he beat her the first time. If he wanted her back, it would have to be the last time.

Most emotional disorders cause an inability to follow my four policies. So before marriage counseling can begin, the emotional disorder must be overcome.

Emotionally disturbed clients often try to convince me and their spouses that if their marriages were fulfilling they'd regain emotional control. I try to convince them that marriage is a two-way street, and until *each* spouse is able to follow my four policies, a marriage can't work. Any emotionally disturbed spouse is temporarily unable to hold up his end of the bargain.

Even after emotions are under control, love units that were withdrawn over the years must be redeposited, or the marriage will remain in ruins. Love is the fuel for marriage, and emotional control simply gets you to the service station.

The couples that I'll describe to you had serious emotional problems that almost ruined their marriages.

The Swinger (Depression)

It was love at first sight. Joy had been invited to a party after work and almost declined because she was so tired. But as soon as she saw Howard, energy seemed to come from nowhere. He was interesting, attractive, and had an incredible sense of humor. By the end of the evening, she knew he was the one.

They dated for about six months. During that time, Joy became acquainted with his family. His parents were divorced and she was unable to meet his father. But his mother, who was remarried, was very warm and welcomed Joy as if she were already her daughter-in-law. When Howard asked Joy to marry him, it felt as if they had known each other all their lives. She eagerly accepted.

The first few months of marriage were great. Howard had a good job, and when his salary was added to Joy's they had more money than they could spend. There were no serious disagreements and they spent quite a bit of time together enjoying their mutual interests.

But they hadn't been married a year before something changed. At first, Howard seemed preoccupied. It was hard for Joy to get his attention and she would have to repeat herself. He seemed to lose his sense of humor. Many of the activities that he'd enjoyed, he no longer found interesting. He even lost interest in sex.

Joy couldn't understand what was happening to Howard. At first, she thought he was getting tired of her and didn't find her as attractive. She tried to compensate by dressing more attractively and putting more romance into their marriage. But the more effort she made, the more he withdrew.

Finally, after work, Howard would just sit in the living room with the lights off, wanting to be left alone. Weekends were no better. Joy begged him to tell her what was bothering him, but he would say nothing.

After several weeks of silence, Howard started to bounce back. He started joking with Joy again and regained interest in the activities that they once enjoyed together. Eventually, he was back to his old self again.

Joy wasn't happy, however. She wanted to know what had happened to him. Even though he was more talkative now, he didn't want to discuss his weeks of self-imposed isolation. So Joy took matters into her own hands and paid a visit to his mother, Grace.

"I've just been through a very strange few months, Grace, and I thought you'd be able to tell me what's going on."

"Oh, I'm sorry to hear that," Grace said with a look of concern. "What would you like to know?"

"Ever since I've known your son, he's been cheerful and friendly. But a few weeks ago he went through something that made him depressed. And he won't tell me about it."

Grace's concern disappeared. "Oh, my! Don't worry about that. Why, Howard's had bouts of depression for years. They last a few weeks and then he's just fine. His father, Ralph, had the very same thing."

"But what makes him depressed?" Joy persisted. "People don't just get depressed for no reason at all!"

"Howard does, and so did his father."

"Why didn't he tell me about this before we were married?" Joy objected.

Grace shrugged. "He's probably ashamed of it. But he shouldn't be—that's just the way he is."

As they continued their conversation, Joy discovered that Grace's husband had suffered a particularly long period of depression, during which Grace had an affair. When her husband discovered it, he divorced her. Grace was embarrassed to admit it to Joy, but felt that she should know now that she was part of the family.

Joy sat Howard down that evening and told him what she'd learned from his mother. Howard was furious. He didn't think his mother had any right meddling in their marriage. He felt

she'd already ruined his father's life and now she was trying to
ruin his. The conversation went nowhere.

Over the next few years, Howard continued to suffer periods of
depression. For several months he'd be cheerful and relatively
carefree, and then there'd be weeks or even months of withdrawal
and unhappiness.

Joy had the sense to know they couldn't have children under
those conditions and that any normal married life was hopeless.
So one day she moved out and filed for divorce.

They saw me for counseling a week later.

It didn't take long to conclude that Howard had a serious case
of recurrent depression that he either inherited or learned from
his father. His intermittent periods of cheerfulness were not
euphoric and irrational, so he simply cycled from a normal state
to a depressed state and then back again. Some people cycle to a
euphoric state of cheerfulness called mania before returning to
depression.

In a private session with Howard, I explained that his emotional disorder, depression, had interfered with his ability to have
a normal marriage. He could not expect to fulfill his wife's
marital needs as long as his condition persisted. However, if he
was willing to overcome this emotional disorder, he would
straighten out a lifelong personal problem and give his marriage
a second chance.

Howard loved Joy very much, and Joy had made it clear that
unless things changed she couldn't remain married to him. So he
agreed to do whatever it would take to get her back.

In consultation with a psychiatrist, Howard began taking a
drug that helped to break the cycles of depression. Within two
weeks, he had adjusted to the medicine, and I spent several more
weeks helping him understand what came over him when he'd
become depressed. I encouraged him to consider antidepressants
the way a diabetic considered insulin: a drug necessary to
compensate for a biological imbalance.

I've been able to help many people overcome depression

without the use of drugs by straightening out a bad relationship or by improving their employment conditions. But when there's evidence of a cyclical depression that doesn't seem related to any event in life, antidepressant drugs may be necessary.

As soon as I was convinced that Howard's cycles of depression were under control, I was ready to work on his marriage.

Howard had violated the policy of honesty from the first day he met Joy. As is the case with many people who suffer emotional disorders, he was ashamed of his lack of emotional control and tried to keep it from her. We spent the first few weeks of counseling clearing up many of Joy's misunderstandings that grew from his dishonesty.

Howard learned to follow all parts of the policy of honesty. First, he learned to share his emotional reactions, even if he thought they were irrational. Then he told Joy about the years that he'd struggled with depression and the devastating effect it had on his self-esteem. He told her how his cycles of depression ruined his ability to follow through on healthy planning, and what his real plans for life were. Little by little, he shared with her feelings that he'd never shared with anyone before.

I explained to Joy that whenever Howard's depressive moods started, his attitudes changed so dramatically that he knew they were irrational and defenseless. That's why he would never explain them to her, even after the depression was over. Now he agreed to tell her how he felt, even if he knew it was irrational.

Howard learned to follow my policy of protection by doing something about the emotional disorder that was driving his wife away from him. His depression had not only made *his* life miserable, it also made *her* life miserable. He had a responsibility to clear up whatever it was about himself that was interfering with her happiness.

He had been too proud to seek professional help for his depression, and his pride left Joy unprotected. But as soon as he was treated with antidepressant drugs, his mood cycles moderated to such an extent that Joy hardly noticed them. He put an end to the erosion of love units that took place during each period of depression.

Howard's emotional disorder had greatly interfered with his ability to follow my policy of care. While depressed, all systems were down and he could not meet Joy's marital needs. But once he overcame his depression, he had little trouble learning how to make her happy. He had already known how to do most of it, but his depression had made it impossible for him to turn his knowledge into practice. Love units started to accumulate once again.

Finally, my policy of time was followed. Before marriage, Howard had no difficulty giving Joy fifteen hours of his undivided attention each week. And when he wasn't depressed, he was able to give her enough time after marriage. But when he was depressed, he just couldn't do it. As he overcame his depression, he was able to consistently give Joy the time she needed.

Joy and Howard are now the proud parents of two children, and their marriage is in great shape. While Howard's emotional disorder is probably inherited, and at least one of his children may some day suffer some of the same symptoms, they'll be in a good position to explain how to compensate and live a happy, productive life. They are outstanding examples to their children of how to overcome an emotional disorder and get on with the adventures of life.

Depression is the most common emotional disorder. If you feel that either you or your spouse suffers from this condition, get professional help. But I should warn you that there are many so-called "professionals" who do not have the ability to help those with depression. If your therapist is unable to help you find relief from depression within a few months, see another therapist.

The Happy Homemaker (Anxiety)

Valerie grew up in a home where emotions were protected, especially fear. Whenever she was afraid of something, her mother encouraged her to avoid it until she felt better. As a result, she missed quite a bit of school. Her mother helped with her studies, so she always had good grades. But she missed out on a lot in life that her parents couldn't make up for as easily.

Chris, a neighbor, grew up with Valerie, and became her only boyfriend. She would invite him over to talk and watch television. Eventually, they became quite attached to each other. She was very attractive and could have dated almost any of the guys at school, but Chris was the only one with whom she felt comfortable.

Chris got a job as a carpenter's apprentice after high school, moved from his home, and rented an apartment. But Val went on to college, and lived at home.

By the time Val graduated, Chris had a good job in construction and had already bought his first home. They had decided not to marry until her education was completed and he was earning enough to support her and a family. That time had come, so they were married.

It would have been relatively easy for Val to find a job, but Chris encouraged her to do whatever would make her happy. So she stayed home and did housework. Val was a terrific homemaker. Meals were imaginative, the home was spotless, and Chris's clothes were always clean and ironed. They had a great relationship at home, sexually and every other way.

They had hoped to raise children right after marriage. However, Val was afraid to stop taking her birth control pills, so five years later they were still without children.

And there was another problem: Val *never* left the house—not even to visit her own parents, or pick up the mail, or water the flowers. Chris knew that she had always been fearful, but he thought she'd grow out of it after their marriage. Now her anxiety was getting worse instead of better.

One day he decided that he'd have to help her turn the corner. "Val," he said casually, "let's go outside for a walk."

Her face froze. "Not today. You know how I feel when I walk outside."

"But you can't live inside a house all your life," he tried to reason. "Besides, I want to be able to go places with you. *I* don't want to live inside a house all my life."

"Well, maybe we'll try it tomorrow. I'm getting sick just thinking about it right now."

"You've become housebound," he pressed. "I don't think you've left the house for three years. Do you realize that?"

"Yes, I realize that," she said desperately. "What do you want me to do about it? Walk out the door and go shopping? I just can't—and you know why."

He blinked. "No, I don't know why. Tell me."

"Because I'm *afraid*, that's why."

"But you and I can never go anywhere together. I'm stuck in this house with you!"

Val burst into tears, and that ended their conversation.

That week Chris went to his doctor for advice, and his doctor referred him to me. As Chris explained his problem, I could see that he'd suffered from the effects of Val's anxiety. He'd been very upset about it but had tried his best to keep his feelings from her since she was so anxious already. Over their five years of marriage he had become increasingly dissatisfied and was considering a divorce.

I explained to Chris that Val's emotional disorder could be overcome. But if it were left untreated, she'd probably be an emotional invalid the rest of her life. It was not only ruining their marriage, but it was ruining her chances for a normal, productive life.

The first step toward her recovery was for him to tell her exactly how he felt. It wasn't in *her* best interest for him to encourage her behavior, and his dishonesty prevented a solution.

After our conversation Chris told Val that he could no longer tolerate her fears of the outside world and that unless she learned to overcome them, their marriage was in serious jeopardy. She didn't take the news well, but he realized that the next move had to be hers.

Later that week, Chris brought Val to my office for her first appointment. It was the first time in three years that she'd been out of her house for more than a few minutes, and she was trembling with fear. She knew that her predisposition toward anxiety had gotten the best of her and that unless she did something soon she would not only lose her husband but all her opportunities in life as well. His threat of leaving gave her the courage to solve a problem that could have been solved years earlier.

With the aid of a psychiatrist, we combined a nonaddicting medicine that helped relieve her anxiety with a program of systematic desensitization. Over a period of several months she learned to spend more and more time outside her home, until she was gone for twelve hours at a time. All with no panic attacks.

Val made a sensational recovery. Before long she had a part-time job. She proved to herself and Chris that her emotional disorder was created, in part, by catering to her anxiety. Her parents had done her no favors by letting her stay home when she feared school, and her husband kept the weakness alive by continuing the policies of her parents.

Needless to say, their marriage rebounded.

Having worked with so many emotionally disturbed people, I'm fully convinced that we do them no favors by pretending that their weakness does not affect us. While it may be rude to tell strangers how they make us feel, if we're in a relationship with someone, we *must* communicate our feelings, *good and bad*. Otherwise the relationship will be superficial at best, and areas of incompatibility will remain.

Chris made his biggest mistake by failing to follow my policy of honesty: He didn't tell Val how he felt about her disability until it was almost too late. Even if he thought nothing could have been done about it, he should have told her how it was affecting him. None of us knows what is possible in life until we try. And honesty clarifies problems so that if there are solutions we're more likely to find them.

Val failed to follow my policies of protection and care. By harboring a known emotional disorder, she failed to protect her husband from the bizarre behavior that it created. She was also unable to meet some of his marital needs because of the roadblocks her fears put in the way. Most recreational activities were impossible and normal social relationships became a thing of the past.

However, once she decided to face her problem, she found she could overcome her fear. Within a year she was off all medication, living a relatively normal life, and happily married.

One observation I've made about marriage and emotional disorders is that, of the three—depression, anxiety, and anger—*anxiety* tends to be the easiest to cure and has the least negative impact on marriage. But our next and final example in this chapter—*anger*, seems to be the most difficult to cure and has the greatest negative impact on marriage. Nonetheless, I've witnessed successful cases, and the following was one of them.

The Monarch (Anger)

One of the traits many women find intolerable in men is indecisiveness. Norm didn't have that problem at all. In fact, he *always* knew what he wanted. And he usually got it, too. So when he met Carolyn and decided she was the one for him, it was only a matter of time before they were married.

Carolyn liked Norm's flair and respected his "take charge" attitude. Since Norm had already decided to marry her, he gave her a great deal of attention and showered her with gifts. She was in love with him in no time at all.

Although he had no reason to be jealous, Norm watched Carolyn closely when she was with other men. She was flattered by his attentiveness and interpreted his jealousy as a sign of his love. But the longer they knew each other, the more possessive he became. Occasionally, he accused her of flirting with other men. Even though she denied it, he didn't believe her and warned her not to do it again.

After they were married, the attention Norm had shown Carolyn before marriage evaporated. He became increasingly demanding, expecting her to cater to his every need, and rewarded her devotion with criticism when something wasn't exactly the way he wanted it.

During their first year of marriage, Carolyn began to realize that Norm had made a career out of winning by intimidation. He had no close friends and he rarely got together with his family. She understood why.

"Norm," she ventured one day, "since we married, you've changed. You're getting to be very hard to live with."

"I think you've changed, too," he shot back instantly. "Where is the beautiful person I dated? You used to care about my feelings. Now all you care about is *yourself.*"

That rocked Carolyn back on her heels! That's how she felt about Norm. Could it be that *she* was the one becoming demanding and self-centered?

Over the next few weeks she tried very hard to make him happy. Whatever Norm demanded she did, cheerfully and to the best of her ability. But it was all one-sided. She met his demands, but he wouldn't meet hers. In fact, if she ever tried to point out the inconsistency he told her to shut up!

Finally, Carolyn decided that all her effort was getting her nowhere and she stopped catering to Norm. That's when the roof caved in. She had tried so hard to make him happy that she hadn't realized what he was like when he *didn't* get his way.

Even though both Carolyn and Norm worked at full-time jobs, she had arranged things so that she could cook dinner and make sure the house was cleaned before he got home. But one afternoon, Norm came home first. When she arrived, he was furious.

"Where on earth have you been!" he demanded.

"Oh, I'm sorry, Norm. There was work that had to be done before I left. I should have called you to let you know I'd be late."

"You didn't have to be late. You could have left the work for tomorrow."

Something in his voice made her very uneasy. "Well, let's forget about it," she said quietly, "I'm home now."

Norm's face was getting red. "No, we won't forget about it. I expect you to be here on time each day. *Is that clear?*"

Now Carolyn was mad. "The only thing that's clear to me, Norm, is that you have no right to *expect* anything. I do things for you because I want to do them, not because you expect them."

"And now you don't *want* to do anything for me. Is that it?"

"Not the way you're acting," she countered. "In fact, I think I'd be happier if I went back to work."

Carolyn grabbed her coat and started for the door. Norm got there first and stood in her way.

"You're not going anywhere. Put your coat away!"

She tried to get past him and out the door, but he pushed her back. As she kept trying to get out of the house, he became more and more violent. First he threw her on the ground. Then he kicked her. Finally, he picked her up and threw her against a wall. When he came to his senses, she was badly beaten, lying on the floor sobbing and covered with blood.

Norm picked up Carolyn and took her to the bedroom where he tried to tell her he was sorry. All she could do was cry. Adding insult to injury, he then forced her to have sex with him.

The next morning, he made her promise that she'd forgiven him and that she wouldn't tell anyone what happened. But as soon as she left the house, she went straight to the police and filed an assault charge against him. From there she went to the hospital for X rays. Then she saw an attorney and filed for divorce.

When Norm finally realized what happened, he called his pastor, who referred him to me.

I've worked with quite a number of husbands who've beaten their wives. I have no time for their excuses. I begin counseling with the observation that hitting anyone is uncivilized, but hitting a woman is cowardly. If a man enjoys fighting, he should fight other men who also enjoy fighting and can defend themselves. Beating a defenseless woman is an outrage.

I explained to Norm that he'd proven he had no business being married to Carolyn. He didn't deserve her. He was nothing but a bully, and Carolyn was smart to have left him.

It has been my experience that if an abusive husband comes for a second appointment after hearing my position on abuse there's a chance I can help him. Norm did come a second time. In fact, he continued to see me for a few months.

During those months we focused attention on anger as an emotion. Anger told Norm to do things that were not only irrational but dangerous to anyone in a relationship with him. Anger told him to demand things of people instead of negotiating. Anger told him to punish people when they refused to meet his demands instead of rewarding people who tried to accommodate him.

Norm loved Carolyn very much and wanted her back, but I explained to him that if he demanded her return, he would be falling back into the old habits that destroyed their marriage in the first place. The way he'd treated her, she had a right to divorce him. The decision to remain married to him was hers, and hers alone.

I made no effort to encourage Carolyn to return to him. She saw me on several occasions, and I let her know that returning would be a big risk. He needed to prove to her that the changes he was making were not just temporary. I also recommended that she should *not* drop the assault charge even if she chose to remain married to him.

I have heard many husbands swear they will never hit their wives again. Many of their wives continue to suffer bruises and broken bones. I've known men who tried to kill their wives after claiming to be "cured" of violent tendencies. One man attempted to kill his wife *three times* before she finally divorced him. He even spent time in prison for her attempted murder.

Unless a man learns to control his temper before marriage counseling begins, no amount of counseling seems to help. He must understand that his anger is his problem and his alone. It makes no difference what his wife does to irritate him or provoke his anger. He has no right to deliberately hurt her.

I encouraged Norm to write Carolyn letters explaining his new insights. He also began to practice controlling his anger in everyday situations in which he was unable to get his way. Finally, I encouraged him to ask her for a date. There was to be nothing romantic about it, just an opportunity to talk to each other.

The date went well, and Carolyn decided to return to Norm if he would see me for marriage counseling. I counseled them together for several months and they made excellent progress. She finally moved back in with him after she'd regained some of the love units that had been lost.

Norm made a complete recovery. And because he learned to control his anger, he was able to follow my policy of protection. He learned that no behavior on Carolyn's part deserved punishment from him. If he was disappointed in something she did, he would simply tell her and try to negotiate a resolution.

He also stopped making demands. He realized that Carolyn owed him nothing and that the efforts she made on his behalf were from her kindness and generosity. As a result he thanked her for the things she did for him instead of criticizing her for failure. He learned the importance of rewards and the inappropriateness of punishment in marriage.

By following all four of my policies Norm and Carolyn were able to build a strong and lasting marriage. Norm's control of his temper made him more successful in other areas of his life as well, especially in his business. Marriage creates great opportunities for self-improvement. If you can make your spouse happy, chances are you've learned some of the most important lessons of life. And the lesson Norm learned not only saved his marriage but made him a much better person.

*   *   *

When someone suffers from one of the three emotional disorders—depression, anxiety, or anger—he cannot follow my policies for successful marriage and, as a result, his marriage suffers. The emotional disorder must be resolved *before* the marriage can be restored.

After an emotional disorder is overcome, the effect it had on marriage remains. All the love units that were lost from violating my policies leave the marriage bankrupt. The love that once made the marriage work no longer exists. It must be recreated.

As with all marital problems, once the source of the problem is eliminated the damage must be repaired. This is accomplished by instating my four policies that once were violated.

In this chapter, I chose three illustrations of emotional disorders where, after achieving emotional control, the couples went on to rebuild their Love Banks. But I know of many others where they've chosen *not* to follow my four policies, the love units were not restored, and the marriages finally ended in divorce. They had the *ability* to save their marriage because they had overcome emotional disorders. But because they had lost their love, they didn't have the *will* to save their marriage.

Love is a precious ingredient in marriage. It makes people *want* to follow my policies. But you *can* follow them, even when love is in short supply. And when you do, love isn't far behind.

Your Marriage Insurance

Fifteen

Deposit Those Love Units!

Those of us in the business of restoring marriages are continually aware of the bliss of a good marriage and the nightmare of a bad one. And we're also aware that nightmare marriages started as blissful marriages. The chance of a blissful marriage becoming a nightmare and ending in divorce is over 50 percent—a staggering statistic. But many of those that do not end in divorce also turn out to be nightmares.

Perhaps one out of five marriages is blissful throughout life. The rest become nightmares, or at least bad dreams. Some cynics don't believe that there are even that many good marriages. But the remarkable truth is that almost all marriages *can* be terrific if spouses would just take better care of each other.

My four policies for successful marriage define what it means to take good care of a spouse. When these policies are followed, bliss will follow.

This book begins with illusions that don't work, illusions that make marriage a nightmare. Interestingly enough, when we take our wedding vows, we're encouraged to recite these illusions that lead to disaster.

The first illusion of marriage is that *the care given and received in marriage is unconditional*. The ineffective policy implied by that illusion is that a spouse can be expected to continue caring, and remain married, regardless of how the other spouse treats him or her. I can expect my wife to care for me, and not divorce me, even if I beat her regularly. This ineffective policy doesn't bring the best out of us; it brings out the worst!

The second illusion of marriage is that *romantic love is permanent*. The ineffective policy implied in that illusion is that romantic love can only occur when people are truly right for each other, and if you're right for each other, you're right for life. Another angle to the same illusion is that romantic love rises and falls by choice. We can *choose* to be in love. Those who have lost the feeling of love have made the choice to do so. This policy implies that love is a commitment, and when my wife has fallen out of love with me, she has broken her marriage commitment. Again, this ineffective policy brings out the worst in us, since it takes love for granted.

The third illusion of marriage is that *a husband and wife should love each other as he or she is, rather than trying to change each other*. The ineffective policy behind this illusion is that accommodation to one another in marriage is unnecessary since a couple is right for each other to begin with. The romantic ideal that marriages are "made in heaven" overlooks the fact that the accommodation of feelings is what brings people to the altar. People change to accommodate each other before marriage. What makes them think they can stop changing after marriage?

With so many illusions, it's no surprise that only 20 percent of marriages turn out to be happy. But obviously I believe that it doesn't have to be that way. Almost all marriages can be happy if they start out with policies that make sense. Those we have now make no sense whatsoever. So let's make some new ones that break through our illusions and set us on the firm ground of reality.

The policies that I created have worked for me in my marriage, and they've worked for thousands of couples I've counseled. The reason they work is that they're designed to deposit love units in Love Banks and keep love units from being withdrawn. My four policies for successful marriage are based on these realities:

1. The agreements made in marriage are conditional. Care is given when it is received.
2. We have very little control over our feelings of romantic love and cannot guarantee it throughout marriage. To a great extent, our spouse controls our feelings, and we control our spouse's feelings of love.
3. Marital needs change over a lifetime, and old abilities may not meet new needs. New needs often require new abilities.

Let's take one final look at my four policies for successful marriage:

The First Policy—Honesty

Reveal to your spouse as much information about yourself as you know: Your thoughts, feelings, habits, likes, dislikes, personal history, daily activities, and plans for the future.

---

1. **Emotional honesty:** Reveal your emotional reactions, both positive and negative, to the events of your life, particularly to your spouse's behavior.
2. **Historical honesty:** Reveal information about all of your personal history, particularly events that demonstrate personal weakness or failure.
3. **Current honesty:** Reveal information about the events of your day. Provide your spouse with a calendar of your

activities, with special emphasis on those that may affect
your spouse.
4. **Future honesty:** Reveal your thoughts and plans regarding future activities and objectives.
5. **Complete honesty:** Do not leave your spouse with a
false impression about your thoughts, feelings, habits,
likes, dislikes, personal history, daily activities, or plans
for the future. Do not deliberately keep personal information from your spouse.

My first policy for successful marriage flies in the face of the
advice given by many in the marriage counseling profession who
often suggest, "What you don't know won't hurt you." My policy
is based on the *truth*, "What you don't know may eventually be
your undoing!"

Honesty assumes that we can solve many of our most important
problems if the information we have to work with is correct. But
when we're given false information we're doomed to failure. I
may feel better for a while living in an illusion, but eventually the
bubble breaks and I find myself defeated. Facts may make me feel
uncomfortable at first, but they help insure my eventual success
and comfort.

Honesty creates the *possibility* of having a successful
marriage. Without it, the other policies are impossible to carry
out effectively. It forms the basis for deciding how to protect and
care. It sets the course; it defines the problem; it organizes
information. It's the starting point.

If you're following this policy, you've told your spouse
everything about yourself that you can remember. In particular,
you're *not* holding anything back. Your spouse knows your
strengths and weaknesses, your successes and failures, and any
events of the past or present that may interfere with your
relationship. If you've ever done anything that would offend
your spouse, or have planned to do anything that would offend
your spouse, you've already revealed it. Your spouse knows you
better than anyone could possibly know you!

The Second Policy—Protection

Do not be the cause of your spouse's pain or discomfort (unless it is unavoidable in order to follow the rule of Honesty).

---

1. **Protection from anger:** Never punish your spouse; never curse, make disrespectful judgments, or lecture through verbal reprimand; express anger as a feeling, not as an instrument of vengeance. Never *intentionally* hurt your spouse.
2. **Protection from annoying habits:** Do not persist in inconsiderate habits or activities. If your spouse tells you that one of your habits or activities is annoying, change it to accommodate your spouse's feelings, or stop doing it. Avoid *unintentionally* hurting or annoying your spouse.
3. **Protection from demands:** Do not demand anything of your spouse that would cause pain or discomfort. When requesting a favor, ask how your spouse feels about doing it, and if the response is negative, withdraw the request.

The policy of protection prevents love units from being withdrawn from the Love Bank. When you keep this rule, love cannot turn to hate.

Sometimes there's a conflict between the policies of honesty and protection. From time to time, your honesty may cause your spouse to experience pain. In that event, the rule of honesty supersedes the rule of protection. In other words, even if love units are lost, honesty should be preserved. These love units are restored when temporary incompatibility is corrected.

Only those with serious anger disorders believe that the correct way to communicate is by screaming, cursing, and hitting! Most of us know that it's a mistake to subject our spouses to our angry reactions, even when they've done something that infuriates us. Protection from anger makes sense to most people.

But it's more difficult to convince people that their spouse needs protection from their annoying habits. Some people have the mistaken impression that there's something sacred about their habits, that they have the *right* to behave as they please. They feel that if their spouse is annoyed by their behavior, the spouse needs to change and learn to accept them as they are. This is one of the most important mistakes made in marriage, and probably the biggest cause of lost love units.

While it's true that eliminating annoying behavior limits your freedom, continuing the annoying behavior limits your love. Annoying habits steal love units away from your Love Bank and can leave you bankrupt! While they may be innocent, not intended to hurt your spouse, they have the same effect as physical abuse and can rob your spouse of love.

If you do something that your spouse finds offensive, don't do it again. If you plan an activity that your spouse will not like, cancel it. Always try to behave in a way that's comfortable to your spouse.

Protecting your spouse from your demands can also be hard to accept. But if you feel you have the right to tell your spouse what to do, you're in trouble. A demand is almost always good for you and bad for your spouse. Otherwise, why would you make it a demand? If it were good for your spouse, it would be a request.

And who's the best judge of what's good for your spouse? Right! Your spouse!

Remember, whenever you demand something that's good for you and bad for your spouse, your spouse should refuse to do it. Why? Because it will take love units away from your spouse's Love Bank.

Never gain love units if it costs your spouse love units. Don't play the zero-sum game, where one of you loses whenever the other one wins. Only play win-win type games, where you both win or you don't play.

While the policy of honesty starts you on the road to marital success, protection sets up guard rails so that you won't weave off the road and crash. The next policy, care, paves the road and directs your efforts to give you the greatest marital reward.

The Third Policy—Care

**Learn to meet your spouse's
most important marital needs.**

1. **Identify marital needs:** Identify your spouse's marital
   needs, and select at least five that are most important to
   your spouse, those that are likely to bring the greatest
   marital happiness and fulfillment.
2. **Meet marital needs:** Create a plan to help you learn to
   meet your spouse's five most important marital needs.
3. **Reassess needs and effectiveness of need fulfillment:**
   Evaluate the success of your plan, creating a new plan if
   the first is unsuccessful. If your spouse finds that a new
   marital need has replaced one of the original five, learn
   to meet that new need.

While honesty prepares you for protection and care, and
protection keeps you from losing love units, *care* is the policy that
gets the love *into* the Love Bank.

To instate the policy of care, a spouse must first understand his
partner's most important marital needs. Once you're skilled in
meeting them, love units pour into the Love Bank.

If you need help in understanding your spouse's marital needs,
or help in becoming skilled in meeting those needs, I strongly
recommend my book, *His Needs, Her Needs*. It's an excellent
guide to following the policy of care.

The marital needs of men and women are very different. This
difference causes a major misdirection of effort. Very innocently,
men think that women need what they need in marriage and try
to meet needs that are important to men. Women do the same
and try to meet needs most important to women.

This misdirection of effort is a major cause of marital dissatisfaction. Not only are the needs left unmet, but all the effort is

unappreciated. Eventually, couples stop *trying* to meet each other's needs, because their most sincere efforts don't work.

But even when men and women understand each other's needs, they still have a problem. Learning to meet a need that you may not have yourself is a very difficult assignment. But it *can* be done, and it *has* been done!

When men and women learn to meet each other's marital needs they become *irresistible*. That's what a successful marriage is all about—love units being continually deposited over the years.

The Fourth Policy—Time

Give your undivided attention to your spouse a minimum of fifteen hours each week, meeting some of your spouse's most important marital needs.

---

1. **Privacy:** The time you plan to be together should not include children, relatives, or friends. Establish privacy so that you are able to give each other undivided attention.
2. **Objectives:** During this time, review and practice the policies of honesty, protection, and care. Create activities that will meet some of the most important marital needs: affection, sexual fulfillment, conversation, and recreational companionship.
3. **Amount:** Choose a number of hours that reflects the quality of your marriage. If your marriage is satisfying to you and your spouse, plan fifteen hours. But if you suffer marital dissatisfaction, plan thirty hours each week or more, until marital satisfaction is achieved. Keep a permanent record of your time together.

The policy of time, like the other three policies, is indispensable for achieving a successful marriage. Honesty, protection, and care can't be implemented without time.

Some couples go to all the trouble of learning how to be honest, how to protect each other, and how to meet each other's marital needs. But then they fail to give each other the hours of undivided attention that they need, and all their effort is wasted.

I once read that the average couple gives each other twenty minutes a week of their undivided attention. That seems to be correct, because whenever I try to encourage a couple to spend fifteen hours a week together, they regard it as a gigantic amount of time. They want to start with one hour, and try to work up to five!

I usually explain that before marriage they had no difficulty finding fifteen hours a week, and without it they would never have fallen in love. How do they think they'll maintain their love on twenty minutes a week?

It's all a matter of priorities. Everyone can find fifteen hours in their week if it's important enough to them. If I paid you one thousand dollars a week to give your spouse fifteen hours of undivided attention, you'd start this week! But no amount of money can replace the love that you need in your marriage. And without sufficient time, all your marital knowledge and skill is worthless.

New Wedding Vows

After all four of my policies are understood, it becomes clear that all four are *essential* in building a successful marriage. Not one can be neglected. With that in mind, I'd like to turn back to the traditional wedding vows that get everybody into so much trouble. If these vows are inappropriate, then what vows should replace them?

The answer: Vows that insure the success of your marriage! Let me propose new wedding vows to you.

Will you have this (man/woman) to be your (husband/wife), to live together in the holy covenant of marriage? Will you be honest with (him/her), sharing your feelings, events of your life, and plans for the future so that you may be understood? Will you protect (him/her), keeping (him/her) from the pain or discomfort of your anger, annoying behavior, and selfish demands? Will you care for (him/her), learning to meet (his/her) most important marital needs? Will you reserve time to give (him/her) enough undivided attention so that (his/her) marital needs can be met? Will you do this as long as you remain in this covenant of marriage?

This vow rules out infidelity, so there's no point in including a promise to be faithful. How can you have an affair if you're being honest and avoiding behavior that causes your spouse pain?

But if you want to include a promise of fidelity, be sure to also include a promise to avoid addiction to drugs and alcohol. And while you're at it, include a promise that when you're overcome by emotional disorders you'll get professional help!

You may notice that the vow doesn't rule out divorce. While I'm very much opposed to divorce, I'm *more* opposed to slavery and oppression. There are many spouses who have violated my four policies so consistently that being married to them is intolerable. A wedding vow, in my opinion, shouldn't commit you to a marriage in which your spouse beats and rapes you in a drunken rage each week. It shouldn't mean that you'll stay married if your spouse leaves you and lives with a lover. It shouldn't force you to tolerate deliberate abuse and neglect.

A marriage vow should commit you to treat your spouse with the highest level of honesty, protection, and care you can muster, *as long as you're married*. If your spouse does the same, your marriage is secure. And what's more important, your *love* for each other is secure!

Eliminating Obstacles to Marital Success

If you've ever been to a seminar on achievement and motivation, the speaker probably impressed you with the importance of setting goals. Such speakers often use the accumulation of money as an example. If becoming a millionaire is your highest priority, you can become a millionaire!

I know that, for most people, the principle works. I've seen high school drop-outs become multimillionaires by dedicating their lives to the accumulation of money. But most have failed in their marriages.

Which would you rather have, a successful marriage or a million dollars? If the answer is a million dollars, you probably won't have a successful marriage.

How about a successful marriage or happy children? Or admiring parents? Or a successful career? Or fulfilling sex? Whatever it is, if it's more important than your marriage, you probably won't have a successful marriage.

One of the most important outcomes in following my four policies is that your marriage becomes your *highest* priority. Nothing can interfere with your efforts to meet your spouse's needs. If you want to have happy children, or admiring parents, or a successful career, or a million dollars, they have to be *secondary* objectives. You can't have them *at the expense of your marriage*. A strong marriage often builds a foundation for the achievement of all these other objectives in life. But these other things rarely build a foundation for marriage.

Make sure you have your priorities straight!

A Marriage Contract

Since most of you who have read this book are already married, my revised wedding vows won't do you much good. So I've prepared a marriage contract that you can sign. This contract goes into effect the moment you sign it. And once it's signed, you've committed yourself to my four policies.

The contract *must* be reciprocal. In other words, both you and your spouse must sign it together, or it won't work.

After the contract is signed, keep this book for its interpretation.

From time to time you may not agree on the meaning of the
rules, so you'll have to refer to chapters 3 through 6 for
clarification. If you still can't agree, find a marriage counselor
who will help you come to an agreement.

Your Marriage
Insurance Contract

THIS AGREEMENT is made this _____ day of
_____, ___ between _____,
hereinafter called "Husband," and _____,
hereinafter called "Wife," whereby it is mutually agreed:

1. The Husband and Wife agree to reveal to each other as much information about themselves as they know by:

    a. Revealing both positive and negative emotional reactions to the events of their lives, particularly each other's behavior;

    b. Revealing information about their personal history, particularly events that demonstrate personal weakness or failure;

    c. Revealing information about the events of their day, particularly those that may affect each other;

    d. Revealing thoughts and plans regarding future activities and objectives;

    e. Never leaving each other with a false impression about their thoughts, feelings, habits, likes, dislikes, personal history, daily activities, or plans for the future; never deliberately keeping personal information from each other.

2. The Husband and Wife agree to avoid being the cause of each other's pain or discomfort (unless it is unavoidable in following section 1) by:

  a. Protecting each other from their angry reactions: Never punishing each other, never cursing, never making disrespectful judgments, or lecturing each other through reprimand; expressing anger as a feeling, not as an instrument of vengeance; never intentionally hurting each other;
  b. Protecting each other from their annoying habits: Overcoming habits or activities that are unpleasant to the other;
  c. Protecting each other from demands: Never expecting each other to do whatever is asked; asking the other how it would affect them and withdrawing the request if it causes pain or discomfort.

3. The Husband and Wife agree to meet each other's most important marital needs by:

  a. Identifying each other's marital needs, and selecting at least five that are most important to the Husband and at least five that are most important to the Wife. These can include any of the following:
    1) Affection: Expressing love in words, cards, gifts, hugs, kisses, and courtesies; creating an environment that clearly and repeatedly expresses love;
    2) Sexual fulfillment: Understanding one's own sexual response, and that of the other; learning to bring out the best of that response in both so that the sexual relationship is satisfying and enjoyable;
    3) Conversation: Setting aside time each day to talk to each other about events of the day, feelings, and plans; avoiding judgmental statements; encouraging informative and pleasant conversation;
    4) Recreational companionship: Developing an interest in the favorite recreational activities of the other, learning to be proficient in them, and becoming the recreational companion associated with the other's most enjoyable moments;

5) Financial support: Assuming responsibility to house, feed, and clothe the family at a standard of living that is acceptable to the other, avoiding long working hours and days spent away from the other;

6) Physical attractiveness: Keeping physically fit with diet and exercise; wearing hair and clothes in a way that the other finds attractive and tasteful;

7) Honesty and openness: Revealing one's own positive and negative feelings, events of one's past, daily schedule, plans for the future; never leaving the other with a false impression; answering every question truthfully and completely;

8) Domestic support: Creating a home that offers a refuge from the stresses of life; managing the home and care of the children in a way that encourages the other to spend time enjoying the family;

9) Family commitment: Scheduling sufficient time and energy to the moral and educational development of the children; reading to them; taking them on frequent outings; educating one's self in appropriate child training methods, and discussing these methods with the other, avoiding any method that does not gain mutual approval;

10) Admiration: Understanding and appreciating the other more than anyone else, never criticizing, but showing profound respect and pride;

b. Creating a plan to help form the new habits that will meet these five needs;

c. Evaluating the success of the plan, creating a new plan if the first is unsuccessful; learning to meet new marital needs if the other replaces any of the original five with new needs.

4. The Husband and Wife agree to give their undivided attention to each other a minimum of fifteen hours each week, meeting some of each other's most important marital needs by:

a. Insuring privacy, planning time together that does not include children, relatives, or friends so that each other's attention is maximized;

b. Using the time to review and practice the policies of honesty, protection, and care; creating activities that will meet some of the most important marital needs: affection, sexual fulfillment, conversation, and recreational companionship;

c. Choosing a number of hours that reflects the quality of marriage: fifteen hours each week if marriage is mutually satisfying, and more time, up to thirty hours each week, if marital dissatisfaction is reported by either husband or wife; keeping a permanent record of time together each week.

5. This agreement is being made under and will be governed by the laws of the state of _____.

IN WITNESS WHEREOF, the parties hereto have signed this agreement on the day and year first above written.

_____ Husband's Signature

_____ Wife's Signature

_____ Witness

_____ Witness